R1-0

① The Parting   9
② The Good Morrow 17
(The World is too much with us 30)
(Kubla Kahn 35)
③ An Irish airman forsees his death 57
(Dulce et Decorum est   76)
④ anyone lived in a pretty how town 79
⑤ To a Small boy who died at Dieppktef Ref. 163   NB
⑥ The Unexploded Bom — 176
⑦ Prayer before birth — 94   NB
⑧ Meeting point — 95   NB
⑨ Meeting of Strangers — 175
⑩ Auto Wreck — 126
⑪ Naming of Parts — 139   NB
⑫ Fern Hill — 104   NB
⑬ Sunstrike — 155

1987

① When in disgrace 14
② My mistresses eyes 16
③ Death be not proud 16
④ Death the leveller 19
⑤ To his coy mistress 21
⑥ Jerusalem 29
⑦ Ode to the west wind 37
⑧ Ode to Autumn 40
⑨ Walking away — 168
⑩ Look Stranger — 90
⑪ They are indeed just lord 55
⑫ My last Dutchess 47
⑬ The Wild Swans at Coole 56

⑭ Constantly risking absurdity   110
⑮ Balm of those who 148
    go forth before daylight
⑯ Lizard   134
⑰ Preludes 71
⑱ Horses on the camargue   83
⑲ Song at Sunrisens   197
    End
⑳ The Sunlight on the 96
    Garden
㉑ Sentry
㉒ Poem in october
㉓ Roy Kloof 168
㉔ The King 132

INSCAPES

INSCAPES

A Collection of
Relevant Verse
compiled by

ROBIN MALAN

Formerly Senior English Teacher,
Cape Town High School, and Director
of PACT Playwork theatre-in-education
company; now Head of English, Waterford-
KaMhlaba School, Swaziland

OXFORD UNIVERSITY PRESS

CAPE TOWN

for D.I.M.K.

Oxford University Press

OXFORD   LONDON   NEW YORK

TORONTO   MELBOURNE   AUCKLAND   NAIROBI

DAR ES SALAAM   CAPE TOWN   KUALA LUMPUR

SINGAPORE   HONG KONG   TOKYO   DELHI

BOMBAY   CALCUTTA   MADRAS   KARACHI

AND ASSOCIATES IN

BEIRUT   BERLIN   IBADAN   MEXICO CITY   NICOSIA

First published 1969

Second impression (revised) 1970

Third impression 1971

Fourth impression 1973

Fifth impression 1975

Sixth impression 1976

Seventh impression 1976

Eighth impression 1976

Ninth impression 1977

Tenth impression 1978

Eleventh impression 1979

Twelfth impression 1980

Thirteenth impression 1982

Fourteenth Impression 1983

Fifteenth Impression 1984

ISBN 0 19 570041 4

OXFORD is a trademark of Oxford University Press

Printed and bound by Citadel Press, Lansdowne, Cape

Published by Oxford University Press, Harrington House, Barrack Street, Cape Town 8001, South Africa

Contents

IN CHRONOLOGICAL ORDER OF AUTHORS

Introduction ix

PART ONE page 1   PART TWO page 111

Acknowledgements 202   *Index of Authors* 205   *Index of Titles* 207

ANONYMOUS   Edward 1   Helen of Kirconnell 2

GEOFFREY CHAUCER (1340–1400)   Introduction to the Prologue 3   The Wife of Bath 5   The Miller 6   Words between the Host and the Miller 6

SIR PHILIP SIDNEY (1554–86)   My true love hath my heart 9

MICHAEL DRAYTON (1563–1631)   The parting 9

CHRISTOPHER MARLOWE (1564–93)   *From* The Tragical History of Doctor Faustus 10   The passionate shepherd to his love 11

SIR WALTER RALEIGH (?1552–1618)   The nymph's reply to the shepherd 12

WILLIAM SHAKESPEARE (1564–1616)   Shall I compare thee to a summer's day? 13   When in disgrace with fortune and men's eyes 14   When to the sessions of sweet silent thought 14   Not marble, nor the gilded monuments 15   Let me not to the marriage of true minds 15   My mistress' eyes are nothing like the sun 16

JOHN DONNE (1573–1631)   Death be not proud 16   At the round earth's imagin'd corners 17   The good morrow 17

ROBERT HERRICK (1591–1674)   To the virgins, to make much of time 18

GEORGE HERBERT (1593–1633)   The collar 18

JAMES SHIRLEY (1596–1666)   Death, the leveller 19

JOHN MILTON (1608–74)   On his blindness 20

SIR RICHARD LOVELACE (1618–58)   To Lucasta, going to the wars 21

ANDREW MARVELL (1621–78)   To his coy mistress 21

ALEXANDER POPE (1688–1744)   *From* The Rape of the Lock 22   *From* An Essay on Man 23

THOMAS GRAY (1716–71)   Elegy written in a country churchyard 24

WILLIAM BLAKE (1757–1827)   The tiger 28   The lamb 28   Jerusalem 29

WILLIAM WORDSWORTH (1770–1850)   London, 1802 30   The world is too much with us 30   Lines composed a few miles above Tintern Abbey 31   Composed upon Westminster Bridge 35

SAMUEL TAYLOR COLERIDGE (1772–1834)   Kubla Khan or, a vision in a dream 35

PERCY BYSSHE SHELLEY (1792–1822)   Ode to the west wind 37

JOHN KEATS (1795–1821)   To autumn 40   Ode on a Grecian urn 41   Ode to a nightingale 42   When I have fears that I may cease to be 45

ALFRED, LORD TENNYSON (1809–92)   Ulysses 45

ROBERT BROWNING (1812–89)   My last duchess 47   The laboratory 49   Prospice 51

WALT WHITMAN (1819–92, U.S.A.)   From Song of Myself 133

MATTHEW ARNOLD (1822–88)   Dover Beach 51

EMILY DICKINSON (1830–86, U.S.A.)   A narrow fellow in the grass 127   A bird came down the walk 130   The bustle in a house 158   I years had been from home 180

THOMAS HARDY (1840–1928)   In time of 'the breaking of nations' 53

GERARD MANLEY HOPKINS (1844–89)   God's grandeur 53   Inversnaid 54   Carrion comfort 54   My own heart let me have more pity on 55   Thou art indeed just, Lord, if I contend with thee 55

A. E. HOUSMAN (1859–1936)   Eight o'clock 56

WILLIAM BUTLER YEATS (1865–1939)   The wild swans at Coole 56   An Irish airman foresees his death 57   The second coming 58   The song of wandering Aengus 183   He wishes for the cloths of heaven 184

LAURENCE BINYON (1869–1943)   History 59

EDGAR LEE MASTERS (1869–1950, U.S.A.)   'Butch' Weldy 156

ROBERT FROST (1875–1964, U.S.A.)   Mending wall 59   After apple-picking 60   Birches 62   Stopping by woods on a snowy evening 63   'Out, out—' 157   The death of the hired man 158

CARL SANDBURG (1878–1967, U.S.A.)   Psalm of those who go forth before daylight 148   Prayers of steel 200

VACHEL LINDSAY (1879–1931, U.S.A.)   A Negro sermon: Simon Legree 172

WILLIAM CARLOS WILLIAMS (1883–1963, U.S.A.)   Heel & toe to the end 121   This is just to say 122   Proletarian portrait 123

D. H. LAWRENCE (1885–1930)   Snake 64   Bat 66   Mountain lion 68   Lizard 134   After the opera 148   Poverty 149   Last lesson of the afternoon 151   The best of school 152   The effort of love 184   Elemental 185

EZRA POUND (1885–1972, U.S.A.)   Alba 186   In a station of the metro 196

JOHN GOULD FLETCHER (1886–1950, U.S.A.)   Crucifixion of the skyscraper 200

RUPERT BROOKE (1887–1915)   Heaven 69   The hill 70   Peace 138

T. S. ELIOT (1888–1965)   Preludes 71   Journey of the Magi 73   Triumphal march 74

JOHN CROWE RANSOM (1888–1974, U.S.A.)   Bells for John Whiteside's daughter 164

CONRAD AIKEN (1889–1973, U.S.A.)   This image or another 117

WILFRED OWEN (1893–1918)   Greater love 75   Dulce et decorum est 76   Anthem for doomed youth 77   Strange meeting 78   The sentry 138

e. e. cummings (1894–1962, U.S.A.) anyone lived in a pretty how town 79
what if a much of a which of a wind 80   somewhere i have never travelled 81
r-p-o-p-h-e-s-s-a-g-r 123   in Just- 187   if up's the word; and a world grows greener
188   i thank You God for most this amazing 190

ROBERT GRAVES (b. 1895)   The cool web 81   Warning to children 115   In broken
images 117   She tells her love while half asleep 186

ROY CAMPBELL (1902–57, S.A.)   The serf 82   The Zulu girl 83   Horses on the
Camargue 83   Tristan da Cunha 85

ALAN PATON (b. 1903, S.A.)   To a small boy who died at Diepkloof Reformatory
163   The discardment 174

WILLIAM PLOMER (1903–73, S.A.)   Shot at sight 120   In the snake park 128   The
wild doves at Louis Trichardt 136

CECIL DAY LEWIS (1904–72)   Come live with me and be my love 88   Let us now
praise famous men 88   A time to dance 89   Walking away 168   The unexploded
bomb 176

A. R. D. FAIRBURN (1904–57, N.Z.)   Song at summer's end 197

H. C. BOSMAN (1905–51, S.A.)   Seed 150

W. H. AUDEN (1907–73)   Look, stranger 90   Musée des Beaux Arts 91   The
unknown citizen 92   Lay your sleeping head 93

LOUIS MACNEICE (1907–63)   Prayer before birth 94   Meeting point 95   The sunlight on the garden 96   Snow 190   Sunday morning 197

EARLE BIRNEY (b. 1908, Can.)   Meeting of strangers 175

STEPHEN SPENDER (b. 1909)   An elementary school classroom in a slum 97   I
think continually of those who were truly great 98   My parents kept me from
children who were rough 169

GEORGE BARKER (b. 1912)   To my mother 174

KARL SHAPIRO (b. 1913, U.S.A.)   Auto wreck 126

R. S. THOMAS (b. 1913)   Autumn on the land 151

M. K. JOSEPH (b. 1914, N.Z.)   On the mountain 143

HENRY REED (b. 1914)   Naming of parts 139

DYLAN THOMAS (1914–53)   And death shall have no dominion 99   Poem in October 100   The hunchback in the park 102   Do not go gentle into that good night 103
Fern Hill 104

JUDITH WRIGHT (b. 1915, Austr.)   Legend 192

THOMAS BLACKBURN (b. 1916)   A small, keen wind 185

ANTHONY DELIUS (b. 1916, S.A.)   Emerald dove 132   The gamblers 150

CHARLES CAUSLEY (b. 1917)   Timothy Winters 170

GUY BUTLER (b. 1918, S.A.)   Cape Coloured batman 105   Stranger to Europe 136
A prayer for all my countrymen 198

ROBERT DEDERICK (b. 1919, S.A.)   Mantis 124   A prayer in the Pentagon 144

LAWRENCE FERLINGHETTI (b. 1919, U.S.A.)   Constantly risking absurdity 116

JOHN HOLLOWAY (b. 1919)   Journey through the night 178

D. J. ENRIGHT (b. 1920)   Blue umbrellas 118

PHILIP LARKIN (b. 1922)   Toads 154   Coming 186

ALAN ROSS (b. 1922)   Secretary bird 131

DANNIE ABSE (b. 1923)   Song of a Hebrew 169

JAMES BRABAZON (b. 1923)   The face on the Turin shroud 191

DAVID HOLBROOK (b. 1923)   Fingers in the door 167

JAMES KIRKUP (b. 1923)   No more Hiroshimas 141

DENISE LEVERTOV (b. 1923, U.S.A.)   The secret 118

SYDNEY CLOUTS (b. 1926, S.A.)   Poetry is death cast out 119   Karroo stop 125
Roy Kloof 168

ELIZABETH JENNINGS (b. 1926)   Florence: design for a city 196

BERNARD KOPS (b. 1926)   Shalom bomb 189

EDWIN BROCK (b. 1927)   When my father died 166

THOM GUNN (b. 1929)   Considering the snail 124   Lines for a book 171   On the
move 193

PETER PORTER (b. 1929, Austr.)   Your attention please 146

TED HUGHES (b. 1930)   Hawk roosting 107   The horses 108   Esther's tomcat 133

JENNY JOSEPH (b. 1932)   Warning 153

DOUGLAS LIVINGSTONE (b. 1932, S.A.)   Leviathan 128   Lake morning in autumn
130   The king 132   Blue stuff 135   Sunstrike 155

C. J. DRIVER (b. 1939, S.A.)   Transvaal afternoon (Part I of In the Lowveld) 134

E. S. BLUMENTHAL (b. 1945, S.A.)   *The earth's atomic death 147   *(Thoughts
written after reading of a mother's suicide) 165

CHRISTOPHER CHEEK (b. 1946)   *Accident 156

ROBERT DAVIES (b. 1946)   *Leather-jackets, bikes and birds 194

LESLIE PICKETT (b. 1946)   *The one that got away 122

NIGEL V. FOGG (b. 1949, S.A.)   *magnolia clinic 166

CHARLES ROM (b. 1949, S.A.)   *Cathedral 181   *I love you well 182   *Though I
be young 182

ELAINE UNTERHALTER (b. 1952, S.A.)   *City people 195

H. D. CARBERRY (W. Ind.)   Epitaph 199

EVAN JONES (W. Ind.)   Lament of the banana man 179

JOHN GILLESPIE MAGEE (Can.)   High flight 140

* indicates written while at school

Introduction

There has to be a reason for the compiling and publishing of this anthology. It is this. Very few anthologies for senior high school pupils in
South Africa have been published in the last twenty years, and fewer
still include any poems written after the end of the Second World War
—and that is twenty-five years ago. This means that the English poetry
of a quarter of a century has gone unread by most South African adoles-
cents. Surely this should not be!

Surely young people should be introduced as completely as possible
to the poetry of their own time? If it is not part of the purpose of English
teachers to encourage senior pupils to read and to experience—and to
write—modern poetry, then it certainly ought to be.

We hear so many people—English teachers not least—complain of
the modern adolescent's lack of 'sensibility', his inability to 'experience',
his spiritual poverty; then we look at the poems we give him to read,
and at least one reason is apparent. Look at the language in which he is
being spoken to. Look at the contexts with which he is being presented.
Too few poems in standard anthologies speak his language or exist in
the context of the world he is living in. Surely one's sensibilities and
awarenesses are developed out of and from the experiences one has,
from the world in which one lives, *first*, before one assimilates the
spiritual experience of a more remote age. If it is sharpening of the
pupils' sensibilities and awarenesses we are concerned with, I am sure
one poem such as Cecil Day Lewis's *Walking away* or David Holbrook's
Fingers in the door is worth five *Lycidases*.

The immediacy of impact and therefore the interest and therefore
the value which the 'sylvan Wyes' and the 'O ye laurels' and the rest
have for a 16- or 17-year-old living in South Africa in the second half of
the twentieth century must be slight indeed until he has come to see,
from a context and a language common to his own, the truths and the
perfection of expression all poetry aims at. Apart from the remoteness
of language, convention and situation encountered in many standard
classical poems, it must surely be encouraging to a pupil to know that
some of the poets he is having presented to him lived in the same
century as he does; and it must be positively heartening to know that
some of them are even actually *alive*.

There is today being formalized in verse a vast store of experience
which does have an immediate impact and a genuine value. A glance

along the shelves of bookshops or through the catalogues of publishing houses indicates that modern poetry is thriving: poets *are* alive—and kicking. There are also, published in Britain, many, rather splendid, anthologies of modern poetry specifically compiled for senior school-children. But, to my knowledge, there is no collection really suitable for all our purposes here in South Africa.

Talking of our purposes, I believe I am correct in suggesting that many English teachers share with me the feeling that our poetry anthologies should be a great deal more than they are and should mean a great deal more than they do. Instead of being the setwork which we and our pupils pick up only to 'study' the thirty-five to forty-five poems prescribed each year, it should be a book which we use and read often, a book which provides us with material to stimulate class discussion and to encourage the reading of poetry, both in class and privately. There should be a large number of modern poems we and our pupils can enjoy and can talk about without having to 'swot them up' and answer examination questions on them. I wonder how many other English teachers have to type out and duplicate sets of modern poems simply to do what none of the current anthologies do—that is, make our pupils aware that every single poet in the English language did not, suddenly and to a man, drop dead in 1945.

This anthology attempts, then, to fulfil our various purposes in the following way:

The book is arranged in two parts. Part One contains, by and large, only the poems, from the anonymous ballads to poems of the mid-twentieth century, which one can with assurance in one's judgement term 'standard' poems. The number of 'classical' poems up to Matthew Arnold has been reduced to a minimum: only those poems from which our prescription selections are drawn year after year have been included. (The only exceptions are a few additional Chaucer extracts which I think give a greater sense of his fun and robustness than those usually selected.) And I do not think that my reduction of the number of 'classical' poems to fifty will be found to be very wrong: most tea-chers will, I am sure, agree that these *are* the poems, from the ballads to *Dover Beach*, which we set most often, discarding the other many thousands of lines of pre-twentieth-century verse most anthologies contain.

From Arnold on, Part One contains the modern poets and poems that have become acknowledged and accepted as 'standard'. Here I have been guided not only by the prescriptions of examining boards but also by general acceptance and taste. It may seem strange at first to find Guy Butler's *Cape Coloured batman* and two poems by Ted Hughes labelled as 'standard' in a school anthology. But general acceptance and taste surely justify their inclusion.

Although I personally have reacted against teaching poetry historically, I have thought it most convenient to adopt a chronological arrangement in Part One.

Then, Part Two. My intention here is to present as many modern poets and poems of as many different kinds as possible: so the selection contains British, American, South African, Australian, New Zealand, Canadian and West Indian poets; Jews, Christians and unbelievers; the socially committed writers, the Beat poets and the Jazz poets; the innovators in form, the free-verse writers, the traditional sonneteers and the modern folk-balladeers; as well as poems written by British and South African writers who were still at school when the poems were written.

It is Part Two that I hope will provide what currently used anthologies lack—the chance for teachers and pupils, in class and privately, to discover, read and talk about modern poetry. As part of the intention of this selection is to discover the variety in modern poetry, the differences in viewpoint, attitude, technique and form, I have seen no point in a chronological arrangement. What I have done is to arrange the poems with a very thin thread of commentary running through the selection. Obviously both the arrangement and the link passages are extremely personal. These commentary links are not intended to be exhaustive textual notes: I have avoided this assiduously. It is my hope that the arrangement and the links will cause two things to happen. First, the pupil who casually flicks through this section of the anthology and reads a particular poem may be stimulated by the link passage to read the poem before or after it, and his interest may snowball in this way. Second, in class discussions, the links—and, indeed, the arrangement itself—may provide opportunities for cross-currents, for argument and debate and disagreement about my juxtaposition of poems or my remarks. Anything which will stimulate our involvement in poetry, anything which will make the school poetry anthology a much-used, much-read book will be fulfilling what I see as the purpose of this book.

I must, having explained the arrangement of the anthology, state as forcefully as I can that the placing of modern poems in each of the two parts in no way implies a critical judgement. It is not intended that poems to be prescribed for study should come only from Part One. It is not intended that the poems in Part One should be regarded as 'those we have to *study*', or that the poems in Part Two should be regarded as 'not really *worth* studying'. I have felt myself bound by no such rigid and academic considerations in the arrangement. For instance, Robert Graves's *Warning to children* is surely as 'standard' a modern poem as one could find, but I have not included it in Part One for the simple reason that it happens to be an ideal poem to introduce Part Two. The relation of Part Two to Part One should be seen as complementary and not supplementary.

The only 'limits' I have used in selection are, firstly, that the poems should have been written in English (though translations from other languages are becoming increasingly popular in modern school anthologies); and, secondly, the limits any compiler is bound within, those of his own taste. I have included only poems which I like and find interesting, and which I feel give a valid account of an experience in poetic form—something which is becoming more flexible and more plain-spoken than it ever was.

If this anthology is found to reflect the age in which we live, and some of the valuable thoughts we think in juxtaposition to those of previous ages, I shall be pleased.

I shall resist the temptation to elaborate upon the choice of the title *Inscapes* further than to say that the word 'inscape' was coined by Gerard Manley Hopkins and has meanings crucial to poetry, literature and art in general. Within this context (or simply by relating the title to the nature of the book), those using this anthology might be allowed first to give their own, very relevant, meanings to 'inscape' before turning to Hopkins and the scholars for their definitions.

Cape Town, 1968   R. M.

NOTE TO THE SECOND IMPRESSION (REVISED)

In this impression we have taken the opportunity of amending the text of the Wilfred Owen poems to that of the C. Day Lewis edition (Chatto & Windus Ltd).

Cape Town, 1970   R.M.

PART ONE

Edward

ANONYMOUS

'Why does your brand sae drop wi' blude,
  Edward, Edward?
Why does your brand sae drop wi' blude,
  And why sae sad gang ye, O?'—
'O I hae kill'd my hawk sae gude,
  Mither, mither;
O I hae kill'd my hawk sae gude,
  And I had nae mair but he, O.'

'Your hawk's blude was never sae red,
  Edward, Edward;
Your hawk's blude was never sae red,
  My dear son, I tell thee, O.'—
'O I hae kill'd my red-roan steed,
  Mither, mither;
O I hae kill'd my red-roan steed,
  That erst was sae fair and free, O.'

'Your steed was auld, and ye hae got mair,
  Edward, Edward;
Your steed was auld, and ye hae got mair;
  Some other dule ye dree, O.'—
'O I hae kill'd my father dear,
  Mither, mither;
O I hae kill'd my father dear,
  Alas, and wae is me, O!'

'And whatten penance will ye dree for that,
  Edward, Edward?
Whatten penance will ye dree for that?
  My dear son, now tell me, O.'—
'I'll set my feet in yonder boat,
  Mither, mither;
I'll set my feet in yonder boat,
  And I'll fare over the sea, O.'

'And what will ye do wi' your tow'rs and your ha',
  Edward, Edward?
And what will ye do wi' your tow'rs and your ha',
  That were sae fair to see, O?'—

'I'll let them stand till they doun fa',
    Mither, mither;
I'll let them stand till they doun fa',
    For here never mair maun I be, O.'

'And what will ye leave to your bairns and your wife,
    Edward, Edward?
And what will ye leave to your bairns and your wife,
    When ye gang owre the sea, O?'—
'The warld's room: let them beg through life,
    Mither, mither;
The warld's room: let them beg through life;
    For them never mair will I see, O.'

'And what will ye leave to your ain mither dear,
    Edward, Edward?
And what will ye leave to your ain mither dear,
    My dear son, now tell me, O?'—
'The curse of hell frae me sall ye bear,
    Mither, mither;
The curse of hell frae me sall ye bear:
    Sic counsels ye gave to me, O!'

Helen of Kirconnell

ANONYMOUS

I wish I were where Helen lies,
Night and day on me she cries;
O that I were where Helen lies,
    On fair Kirconnell lea!

Curst be the heart that thought the thought,
And cursed the hand that fired the shot,
When in my arms burd Helen dropt,
    And died to succour me!

O think na but my heart was sair,
When my Love dropp'd and spak nae mair!
I laid her down wi' meikle care,
    On fair Kirconnell lea.

2

As I went down the water side,
None but my foe to be my guide,
None but my foe to be my guide,
    On fair Kirconnell lea;

I lighted down my sword to draw,
I hackèd him in pieces sma',
I hackèd him in pieces sma',
    For her sake that died for me.

O Helen fair, beyond compare!
I'll mak a garland o' thy hair,
Shall bind my heart for evermair,
    Until the day I dee!

O that I were where Helen lies!
Night and day on me she cries;
Out of my bed she bids me rise,
    Says, 'Haste, and come to me!'

O Helen fair! O Helen chaste!
If I were with thee, I'd be blest,
Where thou lies low and taks thy rest,
    On fair Kirconnell lea.

I wish my grave were growing green,
A winding-sheet drawn owre my een,
And I in Helen's arms lying,
    On fair Kirconnell lea.

I wish I were where Helen lies!
Night and day on me she cries;
And I am weary of the skies,
    For her sake that died for me.

From the Prologue to *The Canterbury Tales*

Introduction

GEOFFREY CHAUCER

  Whan that Aprille with his shoures soote
The droghte of March hath perced to the roote,
And bathed every veyne in swich licour
Of which vertu engendred is the flour;

3

Whan Zephirus eek with his sweete breeth
Inspired hath in every holt and heeth
The tendre croppes, and the yonge sonne
Hath in the Ram his halve cours yronne,
And smale foweles maken melodye,
That slepen al the nyght with open ye
(So priketh hem nature in hir corages);
Thanne longen folk to goon on pilgrimages,
And palmeres for to seken straunge strondes,
To ferne halwes, kowthe in sondry londes;
And specially from every shires ende
Of Engelond to Caunterbury they wende,
The hooly blisful martir for to seke,
That hem hath holpen whan that they were seeke.
   Bifil that in that seson on a day,
In Southwerk at the Tabard as I lay
Redy to wenden on my pilgrymage
To Caunterbury with ful devout corage,
At nyght was come into that hostelrye
Wel nyne and twenty in a compaignye,
Of sondry folk, by aventure yfalle
In felaweshipe, and pilgrimes were they alle,
That toward Caunterbury wolden ryde.
The chambres and the stables weren wyde,
And wel we weren esed atte beste.
And shortly, whan the sonne was to reste,
So hadde I spoken with hem everichon
That I was of hir felaweshipe anon,
And made forward erly for to ryse,
To take oure wey ther as I yow devyse.
   But nathelees, whil I have tyme and space,
Er that I ferther in this tale pace,
Me thynketh it acordaunt to resoun
To telle yow al the condicioun
Of ech of hem, so as it semed me,
And whiche they weren, and of what degree.

From the Prologue to *The Canterbury Tales*

The Wife of Bath

GEOFFREY CHAUCER (tr. Nevill Coghill)

A worthy woman from beside Bath city
Was with us, somewhat deaf, which was a pity.
In making cloth she showed so great a bent
She bettered those of Ypres and of Ghent.
In all the parish not a dame dared stir
Towards the altar steps in front of her,
And if indeed they did, so wrath was she
As to be quite put out of charity.
Her kerchiefs were of finely woven ground;
I dared have sworn they weighed a good ten pound,
The ones she wore on Sunday, on her head.
Her hose were of the finest scarlet red
And gartered tight; her shoes were soft and new.
Bold was her face, handsome, and red in hue.
A worthy woman all her life, what's more
She'd had five husbands, all at the church door,
Apart from other company in youth;
No need just now to speak of that, forsooth.
And she had thrice been to Jerusalem,
Seen many strange rivers and passed over them;
She'd been to Rome and also to Boulogne,
St James of Compostella and Cologne,
And she was skilled in wandering by the way.
She had gap-teeth, set widely, truth to say.
Easily on an ambling horse she sat
Well wimpled up, and on her head a hat
As broad as is a buckler or a shield;
She had a flowing mantle that concealed
Large hips, her heels spurred sharply under that.
In company she liked to laugh and chat
And knew the remedies for love's mischances,
An art in which she knew the oldest dances.

From the Prologue to *The Canterbury Tales*

The Miller

GEOFFREY CHAUCER (tr. Nevill Coghill)

The Miller was a chap of sixteen stone,
A great stout fellow big in brawn and bone.
He did well out of them, for he could go
And win the ram at any wrestling show.
Broad, knotty and short-shouldered, he would boast
He could heave any door off hinge and post,
Or take a run and break it with his head.
His beard, like any sow or fox, was red
And broad as well, as though it were a spade;
And, at its very tip, his nose displayed
A wart on which there stood a tuft of hair
Red as the bristles in an old sow's ear.
His nostrils were as black as they were wide.
He had a sword and buckler at his side,
His mighty mouth was like a furnace door.
A wrangler and buffoon, he had a store
Of tavern stories, filthy in the main.
He was a master-hand at stealing grain.
He felt it with his thumb and thus he knew
Its quality and took three times his due—
A thumb of gold, by God, to gauge an oat!
He wore a hood of blue and a white coat.
He liked to play his bagpipes up and down
And that was how he brought us out of town.

From *The Canterbury Tales*

Words between the Host and the Miller

GEOFFREY CHAUCER (tr. Nevill Coghill)

When we had heard the tale the Knight had told,
Not one among the pilgrims, young or old,
But said it was indeed a noble story
Worthy to be remembered for its glory,
And it especially pleased the gentlefolk.

Our Host began to laugh and swore in joke:
'It's going well, we've opened up the bale;
Now, let me see. Who'll tell another tale?
Upon my soul the game was well begun!
Come on, Sir Monk, and show what can be done;
Repay the Knight a little for his tale!'
   The Miller, very drunk and rather pale,
Was straddled on his horse half-on half-off
And in no mood for manners or to doff
His hood or hat, or wait on any man,
But in a voice like Pilate's he began
To huff and swear. 'By blood and bones and belly,
I've got a noble story I can tell 'ee,
I'll pay the Knight his wages, not the Monk.'
   Our Host perceived at once that he was drunk
And said, 'Now hold on, Robin, dear old brother;
We'll get some better man to tell another;
You wait a bit. Let's have some common sense.'
'God's soul, I won't!' said he. 'At all events
I mean to talk, or else I'll go my way.'
Our Host replied, 'Well, blast you then, you may.
You're just a fool; your wits are overcome.'
   'Now listen,' said the Miller, 'all and some,
To what I have to say. But first I'm bound
To say I'm drunk, I know it by my sound.
And if the words get muddled in my tale
Just put it down to too much Southwark ale.
I mean to tell a legend and a life
Of an old carpenter and of his wife,
And how a student came and set his cap . . .'
   The Reeve looked up and shouted, 'Shut your trap!
Give over with your drunken harlotry.
It is a sin and foolishness', said he,
'To slander any man or bring a scandal
On wives in general. Why can't you handle
Some other tale? There's other things beside.'
   To this the drunken Miller then replied,
'My dear old brother Oswald, such is life.
A man's no cuckold if he has no wife.
For all that, I'm not saying you are one;

There's many virtuous wives, all said and done,
Ever a thousand good for one that's bad,
As well you know yourself, unless you're mad.
What's biting you? Can't I tell stories too?
I've got a wife, Lord knows, as well as you,
Yet for the oxen in my plough, indeed,
I wouldn't take it on me, more than need,
To think myself a cuckold, just because.
I'm pretty sure I'm not, and never was.
One shouldn't be too inquisitive in life
Either about God's secrets, or one's wife.
You'll find God's plenty all you could desire;
Of the remainder, better not enquire.'
    What can I add? The Miller had begun,
He would not hold his peace for anyone,
But told his churl's tale his own way, I fear.
And I regret I must repeat it here,
And so I beg of all who are refined
For God's love not to think me ill-inclined
Or evil in my purpose. I rehearse
Their tales as told, for better or for worse,
For else I should be false to what occurred.
So if this tale had better not be heard,
Just turn the page and choose another sort;
You'll find them here in plenty, long and short;
Many historical, that will profess
Morality, good breeding, saintliness.
Do not blame me if you should choose amiss.
The Miller was a churl, I've told you this,
So was the Reeve, and other some as well,
And harlotry was all they had to tell.
Consider then and hold me free of blame:
And why be serious about a game?

My true love hath my heart

My true love hath my heart and I have his,
   By just exchange one for another given;
I hold his dear, and mine he cannot miss,
   There never was a better bargain driven.
     My true love hath my heart and I have his.

His heart in me keeps him and me in one,
   My heart in him his thoughts and senses guides;
He loves my heart, for once it was his own,
   I cherish his, because in me it bides.
     My true love hath my heart and I have his.

From Idea's Mirrour — Sonnet Cycle
Idea was the name of the lady the sonnets are addressed to. Anne — 2nd daughter of Goodere. No patron.

The parting

Monosyllabic, simple, no imagery
Very ironic

MICHAEL DRAYTON

Since there's no help, come let us kiss and part.
Nay, I have done; you get no more of me,
And I am glad, yea, glad with all my heart,
That thus so cleanly I myself can free;
Shake hands for ever, cancel all our vows,
And when we meet at any time again,
Be it not seen in either of our brows,
That we one jot of former love retain.
Now at the last gasp of Love's latest breath,
When, his pulse failing, Passion speechless lies,
When Faith is kneeling by his bed of death,
And Innocence is closing up his eyes,
Now if thou wouldst, when all have given him over,
From death to life thou mightst him yet recover.

paradox
qualities of love
— moment at Deathbed
Truthful candid note

9

From The Tragical History of Doctor Faustus

CHRISTOPHER MARLOWE

(The clock strikes eleven.)

FAUST.   Ah, Faustus,
Now hast thou but one bare hour to live,
And then thou must be damn'd perpetually!
Stand still, you ever-moving spheres of Heaven,
That time may cease, and midnight never come;
Fair Nature's eye, rise, rise again and make
Perpetual day; or let this hour be but
A year, a month, a week, a natural day
That Faustus may repent and save his soul!
O lente, lente, currite noctis equi!
The stars move still, time runs, the clock will strike,
The Devil will come, and Faustus must be damn'd.
O, I'll leap up to my God! Who pulls me down?
See, see where Christ's blood streams in the firmament!
One drop would save my soul—half a drop: ah, my Christ!
Ah rend not my heart for naming of my Christ!
Yet will I call on him: O spare me, Lucifer—
Where is it now? 'Tis gone; and see, where God
Stretcheth out his arm, and bends his ireful brows!
Mountains and hills come, come and fall on me,
And hide me from the heavy wrath of God!
No! no!
Then will I headlong run into the earth;
Earth gape! O no, it will not harbour me!
You stars that reign'd at my nativity,
Whose influence hath allotted death and hell,
Now draw up Faustus like a foggy mist
Into the entrails of yon labouring clouds,
That, when you vomit forth into the air,
My limbs may issue from your smoky mouths,
So that my soul may but ascend to Heaven!

(The clock strikes the half-hour.)

Ah, half the hour is past! 'Twill all be past anon!

10

O God,
If thou wilt not have mercy on my soul,
Yet for Christ's sake, whose blood hath ransom'd me,
Impose some end to my incessant pain;
Let Faustus live in hell a thousand years—
A hundred thousand, and at last be sav'd!
O, no end is limited to damned souls!
Why wert thou not a creature wanting soul?
Or why is this immortal that thou hast?
Ah, Pythagoras' metempsychosis! were that true,
This soul should fly from me, and I be chang'd
Unto some brutish beast! All beasts are happy,
For, when they die,
Their souls are soon dissolv'd in elements;
But mine must live, still to be plagu'd in hell.
Curst be the parents that engender'd me!
No, Faustus: curse thyself: curse Lucifer
That hath depriv'd thee of the joys of Heaven.

(The clock strikes twelve.)

O, it strikes, it strikes! Now, body, turn to air,
Or Lucifer will bear thee quick to hell.

(Thunder and lightning.)

O soul, be chang'd into little water-drops,
And fall into the ocean—ne'er be found.
My God! my God! look not so fierce on me!

(Enter Devils.)

Adders and serpents, let me breathe awhile!
Ugly hell, gape not! come not, Lucifer!
I'll burn my books!—Ah Mephistophilis!

(Exeunt Devils with Faustus.)

The passionate shepherd to his love

CHRISTOPHER MARLOWE

Come live with me and be my love,
And we will all the pleasures prove,
That hills and valleys, dales and fields,
And all the craggy mountains yields.

11

There we will sit upon the rocks,
And see the shepherds feed their flocks,
By shallow rivers to whose falls
Melodious birds sing madrigals.

And I will make thee beds of roses
With a thousand fragrant posies,
A cap of flowers, and a kirtle
Embroidered all with leaves of myrtle;

A gown made of the finest wool
Which from our pretty lambs we pull;
Fair lined slippers for the cold,
With buckles of the purest gold;

A belt of straw and ivy buds,
With coral clasps and amber studs:
And if these pleasures may thee move,
Come live with me and be my love.

The shepherds' swains shall dance and sing
For thy delight each May morning:
If these delights thy mind may move,
Then live with me and be my love.

The nymph's reply to the shepherd

SIR WALTER RALEIGH

If all the world and love were young,
And truth in every shepherd's tongue,
These pretty pleasures might me move
To live with thee and be thy love.

Time drives the flocks from field to fold,
When rivers rage and rocks grow cold,
And Philomel becometh dumb;
The rest complain of cares to come.

The flowers do fade, and wanton fields
To wayward winter reckoning yields;
A honey tongue, a heart of gall,
Is fancy's spring, but sorrow's fall.

Thy gowns, thy shoes, thy beds of roses,
Thy cap, thy kirtle, and thy posies
Soon break, soon wither, soon forgotten,
In folly ripe, in reason rotten.

Thy belt of straw and ivy buds,
Thy coral clasps and amber studs,
All these in me no means can move
To come to thee and be thy love.

But could youth last and love still breed,
Had joys no date nor age no need,
Then these delights my mind might move
To live with thee and be thy love.

Sonnet XVIII

Shall I compare thee to a summer's day?

WILLIAM SHAKESPEARE

Shall I compare thee to a summer's day?
Thou art more lovely and more temperate:
Rough winds do shake the darling buds of May,
And summer's lease hath all too short a date:
Sometime too hot the eye of heaven shines,
And often is his gold complexion dimm'd;
And every fair from fair sometime declines,
By chance, or nature's changing course untrimm'd;
But thy eternal summer shall not fade,
Nor lose possession of that fair thou ow'st,
Nor shall death brag thou wander'st in his shade,
When in eternal lines to time thou grow'st.
   So long as men can breathe, or eyes can see,
   So long lives this, and this gives life to thee.

Sonnet XXIX

→ IAMBIC PENTAMETER

When in disgrace with fortune and men's eyes

"Power of love" → THEME

WILLIAM SHAKESPEARE

When in disgrace with fortune and men's eyes
I all alone beweep my outcast state,
And trouble deaf heaven with my bootless cries,
And look upon myself, and curse my fate,
Wishing me like to one more rich in hope,
Featur'd like him, like him with friends possess'd,
Desiring this man's art, and that man's scope,
With what I most enjoy contented least;
Yet in these thoughts myself almost despising,
Haply I think on thee,—and then my state,
Like to the lark at break of day arising
From sullen earth, sings hymns at heaven's gate;
  For thy sweet love remember'd such wealth brings
  That then I scorn to change my state with kings.

Sonnet XXX

When to the sessions of sweet silent thought

WILLIAM SHAKESPEARE

When to the sessions of sweet silent thought
I summon up remembrance of things past,
I sigh the lack of many a thing I sought,
And with old woes new wail my dear times' waste:
Then can I drown an eye, unus'd to flow,
For precious friends hid in death's dateless night,
And weep afresh love's long since cancell'd woe,
And moan the expense of many a vanish'd sight:
Then can I grieve at grievances foregone,
And heavily from woe to woe tell o'er
The sad account of fore-bemoaned moan,
Which I new pay as if not paid before.
  But if the while I think on thee, dear friend,
  All losses are restor'd and sorrows end.

Sonnet LV

Not marble, nor the gilded monuments

WILLIAM SHAKESPEARE

Not marble, nor the gilded monuments
Of princes, shall outlive this powerful rime;
But you shall shine more bright in these contents
Than unswept stone, besmear'd with sluttish time.
When wasteful war shall statues overturn,
And broils root out the work of masonry,
Nor Mars his sword nor war's quick fire shall burn
The living record of your memory.
'Gainst death and all-oblivious enmity
Shall you pace forth; your praise shall still find room
Even in the eyes of all posterity
That wear this world out to the ending doom.
    So, till the judgement that yourself arise,
    You live in this, and dwell in lovers' eyes.

Sonnet CXVI

Let me not to the marriage of true minds

WILLIAM SHAKESPEARE

Let me not to the marriage of true minds
Admit impediments. Love is not love
Which alters when it alteration finds,
Or bends with the remover to remove:
O, no! it is an ever-fixed mark,
That looks on tempests and is never shaken;
It is the star to every wandering bark,
Whose worth's unknown, although his height be taken.
Love's not Time's fool, though rosy lips and cheeks
Within his bending sickle's compass come;
Love alters not with his brief hours and weeks,
But bears it out even to the edge of doom.
    If this be error, and upon me prov'd,
    I never writ, nor no man ever lov'd.

→ parody → satirising the sonnets of the time
→ true love → accepts mistress as herself
→ love sonnets — praised mistress → conventional
→ SS mocks extravagant claims made by poets → goes against convent

Sonnet CXXX

→ PROTEST AGAINST INSINCERE COMPARISONS

My mistress' eyes are nothing like the sun

→ Earthy, distasteful diction

WILLIAM SHAKESPEARE

My mistress' eyes are nothing like the sun; → ordinary eyes
Coral is far more red than her lips' red: → sensual
If snow be white, why then her breasts are dun; (dull grey, off-white) — not pure
If hairs be wires, black wires grow on her head. → coarse, black, thick hair
I have seen roses damask'd, red and white, → frankly realistic
But no such roses see I in her cheeks; treatment
And in some perfumes is there more delight
Than in the breath that from my mistress reeks. → strong word
I love to hear her speak, yet well I know → tone gradually becomes more
That music hath a far more pleasing sound:
I grant I never saw a goddess go, — → honest since
My mistress, when she walks, treads on the ground: → sobering, accurate
And yet, by heaven, I think my love as rare → special usage
As any she belied with false compare. → Falsely described with deceit
on comparisons

→ Mockery of convention achieves sincerity, rejects hack
clichés of beauty → total acceptance

Death be not proud

THEME: DON'T FEAR DEATH

JOHN DONNE

→ striking images, intense religious convictions in colloquial terms

Death be not proud, though some have called thee → Death is feared by men
Mighty and dreadful, for thou art not so,
For those, whom thou think'st thou dost overthrow,
Die not, poor death, nor yet canst thou kill me.
From rest and sleep, which but thy pictures be,
Much pleasure, then from thee much more must flow,
And soonest our best men with thee do go,
Rest of their bones, and soul's delivery.
Thou art slave to Fate, Chance, kings, and desperate men,
And dost with poison, war, and sickness dwell,
And poppy or charms can make us sleep as well,
And better than thy stroke; why swell'st thou then?
One short sleep past, we wake eternally,
And death shall be no more; death, thou shalt die.

16

Corinthians I, 4.15

→ ridiculing man's needless fear of death
→ death is a release for the soul

At the round earth's imagin'd corners

JOHN DONNE

At the round earth's imagin'd corners, blow
Your trumpets, Angels, and arise, arise
From death, you numberless infinities
Of souls, and to your scatter'd bodies go,
All whom the flood did, and fire shall o'erthrow,
All whom war, dearth, age, agues, tyrannies,
Despair, law, chance, hath slain, and you whose eyes,
Shall behold God, and never taste death's woe.
But let them sleep, Lord, and me mourn a space,
For, if above all these, my sins abound,
'Tis late to ask abundance of thy grace,
When we are there; here on this lowly ground,
Teach me how to repent; for that's as good
As if thou hadst seal'd my pardon, with thy blood.

10 = 10,15
20 = 10,69
30 = 11,54
40° = 13,05
50 = 15,55

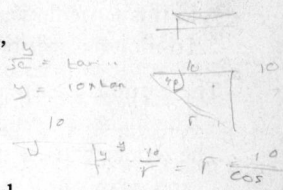

The good morrow

JOHN DONNE

I wonder by my troth, what thou and I
Did, till we lov'd? Were we not wean'd till then?
But suck'd on country pleasures, childishly?
Or snorted we in the seven sleepers' den?
'Twas so; but this, all pleasures fancies be.
If ever any beauty I did see,
Which I desir'd, and got, 'twas but a dream of thee.

And now good-morrow to our waking souls,
Which watch not one another out of fear;
For love all love of other sights controls,
And makes one little room an everywhere.
Let sea-discoverers to new worlds have gone,
Let maps to other, worlds on worlds have shown,
Let us possess one world, each hath one, and is one.

My face in thine eye, thine in mine appears,
And true plain hearts do in the faces rest;
Where can we find two better hemispheres
Without sharp North, without declining West?

17

[Handwritten annotations for "The good morrow":]
→ New world / discovery of love
→ Metaphysical Poem
- Love poem
- Colloquial language - realistic
→ Catholic
→ gay man of world
truly - archaism
→ sense of wonder in love affair
→ refer to classical reference
→ love is greater, more meaningful
→ only grew up when I met you
→ honest, open
→ Finds everything in his lover
of losing one another : strength of love keeps them together
→ paradox - love absorbs / influence
• Time of discovery
• Poetry reflects spirit of adventure
→ They can explore each other
→ Metaphysical
- sincere, open, see each other frankly
- unity - 2 halves = greater intimacy metaphysical, emotionally, spiritually
→ cold
→ sun - end of affair

Combines reason with passion
Conceits - far-fetched images - striking, unusual

What ever dies, was not mixt equally;
If our two loves be one, or thou and I
Love so alike that none do slacken, none can die.

(handwritten annotations: "— Theme: Equality of love — never die — laws of stable proportion"; "same, equal"; "unity"; "love iterating bears equal"; "free hyperbole, conceit paradox, reason & logic .: metaphysical poem")

To the virgins, to make much of time

ROBERT HERRICK

Gather ye Rose-buds while ye may,
    Old Time is still a-flying:
And this same flower that smiles to-day,
    To-morrow will be dying.

The glorious Lamp of Heaven, the Sun,
    The higher he's a-getting;
The sooner will his race be run,
    And nearer he's to setting.

That Age is best, which is the first,
    When Youth and Blood are warmer;
But being spent, the worse, and worst
    Times, still succeed the former.

Then be not coy, but use your time;
    And while ye may, go marry:
For having lost but once your prime,
    You may for ever tarry.

The collar

GEORGE HERBERT

I struck the board and cried, No more.
                I will abroad.
        What? shall I ever sigh and pine?
My lines and life are free; free as the road,
        Loose as the wind, as large as store.
            Shall I be still in suit?
        Have I no harvest but a thorn
        To let me blood, and not restore
        What I have lost with cordial fruit?
                Sure there was wine

Before my sighs did dry it: there was corn
      Before my tears did drown it.
  Is the year only lost to me?
      Have I no bays to crown it?
No flowers, no garlands gay? all blasted?
      All wasted?
  Not so, my heart: but there is fruit,
      And thou hast hands.
    Recover all thy sigh-blown age
On double pleasures: leave thy cold dispute
Of what is fit, and not; forsake thy cage,
      Thy rope of sands,
Which petty thoughts have made, and made to thee
  Good cable, to enforce and draw,
      And be thy law,
  While thou didst wink and wouldst not see.
    Away; take heed:
    I will abroad.
Call in thy death's head there: tie up thy fears.
      He that forbears
    To suit and serve his need,
      Deserves his load.
But as I rav'd and grew more fierce and wild
      At every word,
  Methought I heard one calling, *Child!*
      And I replied, *My Lord.*

Death, the leveller

JAMES SHIRLEY (1596 – 1666)

The glories of our blood and state,
Are shadows, not substantial things;
There is no armour against fate,
Death lays his icy hand on Kings,
    Sceptre and Crown,
    Must tumble down,
And in the dust be equal made,
With the poor crooked scythe and spade.

19

Some men with swords may reap the field
And plant fresh laurels where they kill,
But their strong nerves at last must yield,
 They tame but one another still;
  Early or late,
  They stoop to fate,
And must give up the murmuring breath,
When they pale captives creep to death.

The garlands wither on your brow,
 Then boast no more your mighty deeds,
Upon Death's purple altar now,
 See where the victor-victim bleeds,
  Your heads must come,
  To the <u>cold</u> tomb;
Only the actions of the just
Smell sweet, and blossom in their dust.

On his blindness

JOHN MILTON

When I consider how my light is spent,
Ere half my days, in this dark world and wide,
And that one Talent which is death to hide,
Lodg'd with me useless, though my Soul more bent
To serve therewith my Maker, and present
My true account, lest He returning chide.
'Doth God exact day-labour, light denied?'
I fondly ask. But Patience, to prevent
That murmur, soon replies, 'God doth not need
Either man's work or his own gifts. Who best
Bear his mild yoke, they serve him best. His State
Is Kingly: thousands at his bidding speed
And post o'er Land and Ocean without rest;
They also serve who only stand and wait.'

To Lucasta, going to the wars

SIR RICHARD LOVELACE

Tell me not, Sweet, I am unkind
  That from the nunnery
Of thy chaste breast and quiet mind,
  To war and arms I fly.

True, a new mistress now I chase,
  The first foe in the field;
And with a stronger faith embrace
  A sword, a horse, a shield.

Yet this inconstancy is such
  As you too shall adore;
I could not love thee, Dear, so much
  Lov'd I not Honour more.

To his coy mistress

ANDREW MARVELL

Had we but world enough, and time,
This coyness, Lady, were no crime.
We would sit down and think which way
To walk, and pass our long love's day.
Thou by the Indian Ganges' side
Shouldst rubies find; I by the tide
Of Humber would complain. I would
Love you ten years before the Flood,
And you should, if you please, refuse
Till the conversion of the Jews.
My vegetable love should grow
Vaster than empires, and more slow.
An hundred years should go to praise
Thine eyes, and on thy forehead gaze.
Two hundred to adore each breast,
But thirty thousand to the rest.
An age at least to every part,
And the last age should show your heart.
For, Lady, you deserve this state,
Nor would I love at lower rate.

21

But at my back I always hear
Time's winged chariot hurrying near;
And yonder all before us lie
Deserts of vast eternity.
Thy beauty shall no more be found,
Nor, in thy marble vault, shall sound
My echoing song; then worms shall try
That long preserv'd virginity,
And your quaint honour turn to dust,
And into ashes all my lust:
The grave's a fine and private place,
But none, I think, do there embrace.

Now therefore, while the youthful hue
Sits on thy skin like morning dew,
And while thy willing soul transpires
At every pore with instant fires,
Now let us sport us while we may,
And now, like amorous birds of prey,
Rather at once our time devour,
Than languish in his slow-chapt power.
Let us roll all our strength and all
Our sweetness up into one ball,
And tear our pleasures with rough strife
Thorough the iron gates of life.
Thus, though we cannot make our sun
Stand still, yet we will make him run.

From The Rape of the Lock

ALEXANDER POPE

And now, unveiled, the Toilet stands displayed,
Each silver vase in mystic order laid.
First, robed in white, the nymph intent adores,
With head uncovered, the cosmetic powers.

A heav'nly image in the glass appears,
To that she bends, to that her eyes she rears;
Th' inferior priestess, at her altar's side,
Trembling, begins the sacred rites of pride.
Unnumbered treasures ope at once, and here
The various off'rings of the world appear;
From each she nicely culls with curious toil,
And decks the goddess with the glitt'ring spoil.
This casket India's glowing gems unlocks,
And all Arabia breathes from yonder box.
The tortoise here and elephant unite,
Transformed to combs, the speckled and the white.
Here files of pins extend their shining rows,
Puffs, powders, patches, Bibles, billet-doux.
Now awful beauty puts on all its arms;
The fair each moment rises in her charms,
Repairs her smiles, awakens every grace,
And calls forth all the wonders of her face;
Sees by degrees a purer blush arise,
And keener lightnings quicken in her eyes.
The busy sylphs surround their darling care,
These set the head, and those divide the hair,
Some fold the sleeve, while others plait the gown;
And Betty's praised for labours not her own.

From An Essay on Man

ALEXANDER POPE

Know then thyself, presume not God to scan;
The proper study of mankind is man.
Placed on this isthmus of a middle state,
A being darkly wise, and rudely great:
With too much knowledge for the sceptic side,
With too much weakness for the stoic's pride,
He hangs between; in doubt to act, or rest;
In doubt to deem himself a god, or beast;

In doubt his mind or body to prefer;
Born but to die, and reasoning but to err;
Alike in ignorance, his reason such,
Whether he thinks too little, or too much:
Chaos of Thought and Passion, all confus'd;
Still by himself abus'd, or disabus'd;
Created half to rise, and half to fall;
Great lord of all things, yet a prey to all;
Sole judge of truth, in endless error hurl'd:
The glory, jest, and riddle of the world.

Elegy written in a country churchyard

THOMAS GRAY

The curfew tolls the knell of parting day,
The lowing herd winds slowly o'er the lea,
The ploughman homeward plods his weary way,
And leaves the world to darkness and to me.

Now fades the glimmering landscape on the sight,
And all the air a solemn stillness holds,
Save where the beetle wheels his droning flight,
And drowsy tinklings lull the distant folds;

Save that from yonder ivy-mantled tow'r
The moping owl does to the moon complain
Of such as, wand'ring near her secret bow'r,
Molest her ancient solitary reign.

Beneath those rugged elms, that yew-tree's shade,
Where heaves the turf in many a mould'ring heap,
Each in his narrow cell for ever laid,
The rude forefathers of the hamlet sleep.

The breezy call of incense-breathing Morn,
The swallow twitt'ring from the straw-built shed,
The cock's shrill clarion, or the echoing horn,
No more shall rouse them from their lowly bed.

For them no more the blazing hearth shall burn,
Or busy housewife ply her evening care:
No children run to lisp their sire's return,
Or climb his knees the envied kiss to share.

Oft did the harvest to their sickle yield,
Their furrow oft the stubborn glebe has broke;
How jocund did they drive their team afield!
How bow'd the woods beneath their sturdy stroke!

Let not Ambition mock their useful toil,
Their homely joys, and destiny obscure;
Nor Grandeur hear with a disdainful smile
The short and simple annals of the poor.

The boast of heraldry, the pomp of pow'r,
And all that beauty, all that wealth e'er gave,
Await alike th' inevitable hour:
The paths of glory lead but to the grave.

Nor you, ye Proud, impute to these the fault,
If Mem'ry o'er their tomb no trophies raise,
Where thro' the long-drawn aisle and fretted vault
The pealing anthem swells the note of praise.

Can storied urn or animated bust
Back to its mansion call the fleeting breath?
Can Honour's voice provoke the silent dust,
Or Flatt'ry soothe the dull cold ear of Death?

Perhaps in this neglected spot is laid
Some heart once pregnant with celestial fire;
Hands, that the rod of empire might have sway'd,
Or wak'd to ecstasy the living lyre.

But Knowledge to their eyes her ample page
Rich with the spoils of time did ne'er unroll;
Chill Penury repress'd their noble rage,
And froze the genial current of the soul.

Full many a gem of purest ray serene
The dark unfathom'd caves of ocean bear:
Full many a flower is born to blush unseen,
And waste its sweetness on the desert air.

Some village Hampden, that with dauntless breast
The little Tyrant of his fields withstood;
Some mute inglorious Milton here may rest,
Some Cromwell guiltless of his country's blood.

Th' applause of list'ning senates to command,
The threats of pain and ruin to despise,
To scatter plenty o'er a smiling land,
And read their hist'ry in a nation's eyes,

Their lot forbade: nor circumscrib'd alone
Their growing virtues, but their crimes confin'd,
Forbade to wade through slaughter to a throne,
And shut the gates of mercy on mankind,

The struggling pangs of conscious truth to hide,
To quench the blushes of ingenuous shame,
Or heap the shrine of Luxury and Pride
With incense kindled at the Muse's flame.

Far from the madding crowd's ignoble strife,
Their sober wishes never learn'd to stray;
Along the cool sequester'd vale of life
They kept the noiseless tenor of their way.

Yet ev'n these bones from insult to protect
Some frail memorial still erected nigh,
With uncouth rhymes and shapeless sculpture deck'd,
Implores the passing tribute of a sigh.

Their name, their years, spelt by th' unletter'd Muse,
The place of fame and elegy supply:
And many a holy text around she strews,
That teach the rustic moralist to die.

For who, to dumb Forgetfulness a prey,
This pleasing anxious being e'er resign'd,
Left the warm precincts of the cheerful day,
Nor cast one longing ling'ring look behind?

On some fond breast the parting soul relies,
Some pious drops the closing eye requires;
Ev'n from the tomb the voice of Nature cries,
Ev'n in our ashes live their wonted fires.

For thee, who mindful of th' unhonour'd Dead,
Dost in these lines their artless tale relate;
If chance, by lonely Contemplation led,
Some kindred Spirit shall inquire thy fate,

Haply some hoary-headed swain may say,
'Oft have we seen him at the peep of dawn
Brushing with hasty steps the dews away
To meet the sun upon the upland lawn.

'There at the foot of yonder nodding beech
That wreathes its old fantastic roots so high,
His listless length at noontide would he stretch,
And pore upon the brook that babbles by.

'Hard by yon wood, now smiling as in scorn,
Mutt'ring his wayward fancies he would rove;
Now drooping, woeful wan, like one forlorn,
Or crazed with care, or cross'd in hopeless love.

'One morn I miss'd him on the custom'd hill,
Along the heath and near his fav'rite tree;
Another came; nor yet beside the rill,
Nor up the lawn, nor at the wood was he;

'The next, with dirges due in sad array
Slow thro' the church-way path we saw him borne.
Approach and read (for thou canst read) the lay
Grav'd on the stone beneath yon aged thorn.'

The Epitaph

Here rests his head upon the lap of Earth
A youth to Fortune and to Fame unknown.
Fair Science frowned not on his humble birth,
And Melancholy marked him for her own.

Large was his bounty, and his soul sincere,
Heav'n did a recompense as largely send:
He gave to Mis'ry all he had, a tear,
He gain'd from Heav'n ('twas all he wish'd) a friend.

No farther seek his merits to disclose,
Or draw his frailties from their dread abode,
(There they alike in trembling hope repose,)
The bosom of his Father and his God.

The tiger

WILLIAM BLAKE

Tiger! Tiger! burning bright
In the forests of the night,
What immortal hand or eye
Could frame thy fearful symmetry?

In what distant deeps or skies
Burnt the fire of thine eyes?
On what wings dare he aspire?
What the hand dare seize the fire?

And what shoulder, and what art,
Could twist the sinews of thy heart?
And when thy heart began to beat,
What dread hand? and what dread feet?

What the hammer? what the chain?
In what furnace was thy brain?
What the anvil? what dread grasp
Dare its deadly terrors clasp?

When the stars threw down their spears,
And water'd heaven with their tears,
Did he smile his work to see?
Did he who made the Lamb make thee?

Tiger! Tiger! burning bright
In the forests of the night,
What immortal hand or eye
Dare frame thy fearful symmetry?

The lamb

WILLIAM BLAKE

Little Lamb, who made thee?
Dost thou know who made thee?
Gave thee life, and bid thee feed,
By the stream and o'er the mead;

Gave thee clothing of delight,
Softest clothing, woolly, bright;
Gave thee such a tender voice,
Making all the vales rejoice?
    Little Lamb, who made thee?
    Dost thou know who made thee?

    Little Lamb, I'll tell thee,
    Little Lamb, I'll tell thee:
He is callèd by thy name,
For He calls Himself a Lamb.
He is meek, and He is mild;
He became a little child.
I a child, and thou a lamb,
We are callèd by His name.
    Little Lamb, God bless thee!
    Little Lamb, God bless thee!

Jerusalem

WILLIAM BLAKE

And did those feet in ancient time
    Walk upon England's mountains green?
And was the holy Lamb of God
    On England's pleasant pastures seen?

And did the Countenance Divine
    Shine forth upon our clouded hills?
And was Jerusalem builded here
    Among these dark Satanic Mills?

Bring me my bow of burning gold!
    Bring me my arrows of desire!
Bring me my spear! O clouds, unfold!
    Bring me my chariot of fire!

I will not cease from mental fight,
    Nor shall my sword sleep in my hand.
Till we have built Jerusalem
    In England's green and pleasant land.

29

London, 1802

Milton! thou shouldst be living at this hour:
England hath need of thee: she is a fen
Of stagnant waters: altar, sword, and pen,
Fireside, the heroic wealth of hall and bower,
Have forfeited their ancient English dower
Of inward happiness. We are selfish men;
Oh! raise us up, return to us again;
And give us manners, virtue, freedom, power.
Thy soul was like a Star, and dwelt apart;
Thou hadst a voice whose sound was like the sea:
Pure as the naked heavens, majestic, free,
So didst thou travel on life's common way,
In cheerful godliness; and yet thy heart
The lowliest duties on herself did lay.

[handwritten notes:]
- Patrachan sonnet → Octave & Sestet
- IR - wanted to return to nature
- Romantics - subjective
  - attitude of child
  - simple, innocent, spontaneous, uninhibited

The world is too much with us

[handwritten: → Romantic, pantheist - sees God in Nature]

The world is too much with us; late and soon,
Getting and spending, we lay waste our powers:
Little we see in Nature that is ours;
We have given our hearts away, a sordid boon!
This Sea that bares her bosom to the moon;
The winds that will be howling at all hours,
And are up-gathered now like sleeping flowers;
For this, for everything, we are out of tune;
It moves us not.—Great God! I'd rather be
A Pagan suckled in a creed outworn;
So might I, standing on this pleasant lea,
Have glimpses that would make me less forlorn;
Have sight of Proteus rising from the sea;
Or hear old Triton blow his wreathèd horn.

30

Lines composed a few miles above Tintern Abbey

WILLIAM WORDSWORTH

Five years have passed; five summers, with the length
Of five long winters! and again I hear
These waters, rolling from their mountain-springs
With a soft inland murmur.—Once again
Do I behold these steep and lofty cliffs,
That on a wild secluded scene impress
Thoughts of more deep seclusion; and connect
The landscape with the quiet of the sky.
The day is come when I again repose
Here, under this dark sycamore, and view
These plots of cottage-ground, these orchard-tufts,
Which at this season, with their unripe fruits,
Are clad in one green hue, and lose themselves
'Mid groves and copses. Once again I see
These hedge-rows, hardly hedge-rows, little lines
Of sportive wood run wild: these pastoral farms,
Green to the very door; and wreaths of smoke
Sent up, in silence, from among the trees!
With some uncertain notice, as might seem
Of vagrant dwellers in the houseless woods,
Or of some Hermit's cave, where by his fire
The Hermit sits alone.
                          These beauteous forms,
Through a long absence, have not been to me
As is a landscape to a blind man's eye:
But oft, in lonely rooms, and 'mid the din
Of towns and cities, I have owed to them,
In hours of weariness, sensations sweet,
Felt in the blood, and felt along the heart;
And passing even into my purer mind,
With tranquil restoration:—feelings too
Of unremembered pleasure: such, perhaps,
As have no slight or trivial influence
On that best portion of a good man's life,
His little, nameless, unremembered, acts
Of kindness and of love. Nor less, I trust,
To them I may have owed another gift,

Of aspect more sublime; that blessed mood,
In which the burthen of the mystery,
In which the heavy and the weary weight
Of all this unintelligible world,
Is lightened:—that serene and blessed mood,
In which the affections gently lead us on,—
Until, the breath of this corporeal frame
And even the motion of our human blood
Almost suspended, we are laid asleep
In body, and become a living soul:
While with an eye made quiet by the power
Of harmony, and the deep power of joy,
We see into the life of things.
                                        If this
Be but a vain belief, yet, oh! how oft—
In darkness and amid the many shapes
Of joyless daylight; when the fretful stir
Unprofitable, and the fever of the world,
Have hung upon the beatings of my heart—
How oft, in spirit, have I turned to thee,
O silvan Wye! thou wanderer thro' the woods,
How often has my spirit turned to thee!
And now, with gleams of half-extinguished thought,
With many recognitions dim and faint,
And somewhat of a sad perplexity,
The picture of the mind revives again:
While here I stand, not only with the sense
Of present pleasure, but with pleasing thoughts
That in this moment there is life and food
For future years. And so I dare to hope,
Though changed, no doubt, from what I was when first
I came among these hills; when like a roe
I bounded o'er the mountains, by the sides
Of the deep rivers, and the lonely streams,
Wherever nature led: more like a man
Flying from something that he dreads than one
Who sought the thing he loved. For nature then
(The coarser pleasure of my boyish days,
And their glad animal movements all gone by)
To me was all in all.—I cannot paint

What then I was. The sounding cataract
Haunted me like a passion: the tall rock,
The mountain, and the deep and gloomy wood,
Their colours and their forms, were then to me
An appetite; a feeling and a love,
That had no need of a remoter charm,
By thought supplied, nor any interest
Unborrowed from the eye.—That time is past,
And all its aching joys are now no more,
And all its dizzy raptures. Not for this
Faint I, nor mourn nor murmur; other gifts
Have followed; for such loss, I would believe,
Abundant recompense. For I have learned
To look on nature, not as in the hour
Of thoughtless youth; but hearing oftentimes
The still, sad music of humanity,
Nor harsh nor grating, though of ample power
To chasten and subdue. And I have felt
A presence that disturbs me with the joy
Of elevated thoughts; a sense sublime
Of something far more deeply interfused,
Whose dwelling is the light of setting suns,
And the round ocean and the living air,
And the blue sky, and in the mind of man:
A motion and a spirit, that impels
All thinking things, all objects of all thought,
And rolls through all things. Therefore am I still
A lover of the meadows and the woods,
And mountains; and of all that we behold
From this green earth; of all the mighty world
Of eye, and ear,—both what they half-create,
And what perceive; well pleased to recognise
In nature and the language of the sense
The anchor of my purest thoughts, the nurse,
The guide, the guardian of my heart, and soul
Of all my moral being.
            Nor perchance,
If I were not thus taught, should I the more
Suffer my genial spirits to decay:
For thou art with me here upon the banks

Of this fair river; thou my dearest Friend,
My dear, dear Friend; and in thy voice I catch
The language of my former heart, and read
My former pleasures in the shooting lights
Of thy wild eyes. Oh! yet a little while
May I behold in thee what I was once,
My dear, dear Sister! and this prayer I make,
Knowing that Nature never did betray
The heart that loved her; 'tis her privilege,
Through all the years of this our life, to lead
From joy to joy: for she can so inform
The mind that is within us, so impress
With quietness and beauty, and so feed
With lofty thoughts, that neither evil tongues,
Rash judgments, nor the sneers of selfish men,
Nor greetings where no kindness is, nor all
The dreary intercourse of daily life,
Shall e'er prevail against us, or disturb
Our cheerful faith, that all which we behold
Is full of blessings. Therefore let the moon
Shine on thee in thy solitary walk;
And let the misty mountain-winds be free
To blow against thee: and, in after-years,
When these wild ecstasies shall be matured
Into a sober pleasure; when thy mind
Shall be a mansion for all lovely forms,
Thy memory be as a dwelling-place
For all sweet sounds and harmonies; oh! then,
If solitude, or fear, or pain, or grief,
Should be thy portion, with what healing thoughts
Of tender joy wilt thou remember me,
And these my exhortations! Nor, perchance—
If I should be where I no more can hear
Thy voice, nor catch from thy wild eyes these gleams
Of past existence—wilt thou then forget
That on the banks of this delightful stream
We stood together; and that I, so long
A worshipper of Nature, hither came
Unwearied in that service: rather say
With warmer love—oh! with far deeper zeal

Of holier love. Nor wilt thou then forget,
That after many wanderings, many years
Of absence, these steep woods and lofty cliffs,
And this green pastoral landscape, were to me
More dear, both for themselves and for thy sake!

Composed upon Westminster Bridge

WILLIAM WORDSWORTH

Earth has not anything to show more fair:
Dull would he be of soul who could pass by
A sight so touching in its majesty:
This City now doth, like a garment, wear
The beauty of the morning: silent, bare
Ships, towers, domes, theatres, and temples lie
Open unto the fields, and to the sky;
All bright and glittering in the smokeless air.
Never did sun more beautifully steep
In his first splendour, valley, rock, or hill;
Ne'er saw I, never felt, a calm so deep!
The river glideth at his own sweet will:
Dear God! the very houses seem asleep;
And all that mighty heart is lying still!

[handwritten annotations:]
- painful disease - took morphine - became addicted - "high"
- In bed - reading book about East - sleeps - thinks up poem - wakes up
- starts writing down & disturbed

- imagination
- creation of art, life
- Very symbolic

Kubla Khan or, a vision in a dream

[handwritten: mans urge to create dream world / visionary poem]

A FRAGMENT

SAMUEL TAYLOR COLERIDGE

[handwritten: visionary poem / worked with Wordsworth / - supernatural]

[handwritten: exotic, far-away / imagination / eternal life]

In Xanadu did Kubla Khan
A stately pleasure-dome decree:
Where Alph, the sacred river, ran
Through caverns measureless to man
  Down to a sunless sea.
So twice five miles of fertile ground
With walls and towers were girdled round:

[handwritten annotations: God, God-like King, anyone who creates / art, any creator / work of art, life, earth, anything created / ordained - like God - act of creation / beginning, start, source of life, birth to death, stream of time / time - stream of life / infinity, art & creation is infinite / true art combines pleasure & imagination / Death / large, endless / imagination - of artist, God, any creator / description]

35

[Handwritten top margin: River of life runs through fertile imagination | Garden of Eden | Paradise — universalises state creating paranomic symbol of man & nature]

And here were gardens bright with sinuous rills, *[life streams ① Imagination of River ② Garden of Eden]*
Where blossomed many an incense-bearing tree;
And here were forests ancient as the hills,
Enfolding sunny spots of greenery. *[blends sacred, romantic, satanic]*

[Rivers origin related to height & chasm — commenting on man's images ideas and | Sex — high romantic & cheap dirty + his society was unpermissive]

But oh! that deep romantic chasm which slanted *[mystic glamour of sex]*
Down the green hill athwart a cedarn cover! *[Lorman's Tree — sex — image of creative]*
A savage place! as holy and enchanted *[lunacy — creation of life | art | universe]*
As e'er beneath a waning moon was haunted *[strong message — "CREATIVE PROCESS"]*
By woman wailing for her demon-lover! *[something evil]*
And from this chasm, with ceaseless turmoil seething, *[despite taboos sb'll produce creature / erotic — creation of]*
As if this earth in fast thick pants were breathing, *[images of birth | creation]*
A mighty fountain momently was forced: *[suggest power & strength]*
Amid whose swift half-intermitted burst *[Orgasm or sexy creation]*
Huge fragments vaulted like rebounding hail, *[Energy needed to create]*
Or chaffy grain beneath the thresher's flail:
And mid these dancing rocks at once and ever *[personification]*
It flung up momently the sacred river. *[life | art | earth]*
Five miles meandering with a mazy motion *[uncertain / valley — alliteration onomatopoeia — love, uncertain, blind process]*
Through wood and dale the sacred river ran, *[life — Enigma, mystery of life — creation followed by life]*
Then reached the caverns measureless to man, *[death, infinity, nothing]*
And sank in tumult to a lifeless ocean: *[died / agony / ocean]*
And 'mid this tumult Kubla heard from far *[noise / confusion — leads to war, appropriate]*
Ancestral voices prophesying war! *[Napoleonic war — war leads to death]*

[past ancestral worship / instinct — idea to create — NB to protect dome — symbol of creation — what is created — from outside world]

The shadow of the dome of pleasure *[shorter, lighter, different metre]*
Floated midway on the waves; *[halfway / birth & death]*
Where was heard the mingled measure *[alliteration]*
From the fountain and the caves. *[source / birth — death, 'caverns measureless to man']*
It was a miracle of rare device, *[art, not many people — art transcends ideas of finite etc.]*
A sunny pleasure-dome with caves of ice! *[pleasure — death — paradox, antithesis — art has death, comes from beneath — life / heat]*

A damsel with a dulcimer *[musical instrument]*
In a vision once I saw: *[first person]*
It was an Abyssinian maid,
And on her dulcimer she played, *[music — art, poetry]*
Singing of Mount Abora. *[literary association — Milton — Mount Amara, Abyssinia where kings secluded]*
Could I revive within me *[elliptic]*
Her symphony and song,
To such a deep delight 'twould win me, *[lines longer, drawn out]*

36

That with music loud and long,
I would build that dome in air,
That sunny dome! those caves of ice!
And all who heard should see them there,
And all should cry, Beware! Beware!
His flashing eyes, his floating hair!
Weave a circle round him thrice,
And close your eyes with holy dread,
For he on honey-dew hath fed,
And drank the milk of Paradise.

Ode to the west wind

PERCY BYSSHE SHELLEY

I

O wild West Wind, thou breath of Autumn's being,
Thou, from whose unseen presence the leaves dead
Are driven, like ghosts from an enchanter fleeing,

Yellow, and black, and pale, and hectic red,
Pestilence-stricken multitudes: O thou,
Who chariotest to their dark wintry bed

The wingèd seeds, where they lie cold and low,
Each like a corpse within its grave, until
Thine azure sister of the Spring shall blow

Her clarion o'er the dreaming earth, and fill
(Driving sweet buds like flocks to feed in air)
With living hues and odours plain and hill:

Wild Spirit, which art moving everywhere;
Destroyer and preserver; hear, oh, hear!

II AIR

Thou on whose stream, 'mid the steep sky's commotion,
Loose clouds like earth's decaying leaves are shed,
Shook from the tangled boughs of Heaven and Ocean,

Angels of rain and lightning: there are spread
On the blue surface of thine aëry surge,
Like the bright hair uplifted from the head

Of some fierce Maenad, even from the dim verge
Of the horizon to the zenith's height,
The locks of the approaching storm. Thou dirge

Of the dying year, to which this closing night
Will be the dome of a vast sepulchre,
Vaulted with all thy congregated might

Of vapours, from whose solid atmosphere
Black rain, and fire, and hail will burst: oh, hear!

III WATER

Thou who didst waken from his summer dreams
The blue Mediterranean, where he lay,
Lulled by the coil of his crystalline streams,

Beside a pumice isle in Baiae's bay,
And saw in sleep old palaces and towers
Quivering within the wave's intenser day,

All overgrown with azure moss and flowers
So sweet, the sense faints picturing them! Thou
For whose path the Atlantic's level powers

Cleave themselves into chasms, while far below
The sea-blooms and the oozy woods which wear
The sapless foliage of the ocean, know

Thy voice, and suddenly grow grey with fear,
And tremble and despoil themselves: oh, hear!

IV

If I were a dead leaf thou mightest bear;
If I were a swift cloud to fly with thee;
A wave to pant beneath thy power, and share

The impulse of thy strength, only less free
Than thou, O uncontrollable! If even
I were as in my boyhood, and could be

The comrade of thy wanderings over Heaven,
As then, when to outstrip thy skiey speed
Scarce seemed a vision; I would ne'er have striven

As thus with thee in prayer in my sore need.
Oh, lift me as a wave, a leaf, a cloud!
I fall upon the thorns of life! I bleed!

A heavy weight of hours has chained and bowed
One too like thee: tameless, and swift, and proud.

V

Make me thy lyre, even as the forest is:
What if my leaves are falling like its own!
The tumult of thy mighty harmonies

Will take from both a deep, autumnal tone,
Sweet though in sadness. Be thou, Spirit fierce,
My spirit! Be thou me, impetuous one!

Drive my dead thoughts over the universe
Like withered leaves to quicken a new birth!
And, by the incantation of this verse,

Scatter, as from an unextinguished hearth
Ashes and sparks, my words among mankind!
Be through my lips to unawakened earth

The trumpet of a prophecy! O, Wind,
If Winter comes, can Spring be far behind?

39

To autumn

JOHN KEATS

I

Season of mists and mellow fruitfulness,
    Close bosom-friend of the maturing sun;
Conspiring with him how to load and bless
    With fruit the vines that round the thatch-eves run;
To bend with apples the moss'd cottage-trees,
    And fill all fruit with ripeness to the core;
        To swell the gourd, and plump the hazel shells
With a sweet kernel; to set budding more,
    And still more, later flowers for the bees,
    Until they think warm days will never cease,
        For summer has o'er-brimm'd their clammy cells.

II

Who hath not seen thee oft amid thy store?
    Sometimes whoever seeks abroad may find
Thee sitting careless on a granary floor,
    Thy hair soft-lifted by the winnowing wind;
Or on a half-reap'd furrow sound asleep,
    Drows'd with the fume of poppies, while thy hook
        Spares the next swath and all its twined flowers:
And sometimes like a gleaner thou dost keep
    Steady thy laden head across a brook;
    Or by a cyder-press, with patient look,
        Thou watchest the last oozings hours by hours.

III

Where are the songs of Spring? Aye, where are they?
    Think not of them, thou hast thy music too,—
While barred clouds bloom the soft-dying day,
    And touch the stubble-plains with rosy hue;
Then in a wailful choir the small gnats mourn
    Among the river-sallows, borne aloft
        Or sinking as the light wind lives or dies;
And full-grown lambs loud bleat from hilly bourn;
    Hedge-crickets sing; and now with treble soft
    The red-breast whistles from a garden-croft;
        And gathering swallows twitter in the skies.

40

Ode on a Grecian urn

JOHN KEATS

I

Thou still unravish'd bride of quietness,
  Thou foster-child of silence and slow time,
Sylvan historian, who canst thus express
  A flowery tale more sweetly than our rhyme:
What leaf-fring'd legend haunts about thy shape
    Of deities or mortals, or of both,
      In Tempe or the dale of Arcady?
What men or gods are these? What maidens loth?
    What mad pursuit? What struggle to escape?
      What pipes and timbrels? What wild ecstasy?

II

Heard melodies are sweet, but those unheard
  Are sweeter; therefore, ye soft pipes, play on;
Not to the sensual ear, but, more endear'd,
  Pipe to the spirit ditties of no tone:
Fair youth, beneath the trees, thou canst not leave
    Thy song, nor ever can those trees be bare;
      Bold Lover, never, never canst thou kiss,
Though winning near the goal—yet, do not grieve;
    She cannot fade, though thou hast not thy bliss,
      For ever wilt thou love, and she be fair!

III

Ah, happy, happy boughs! that cannot shed
  Your leaves, nor ever bid the Spring adieu;
And, happy melodist, unwearied,
  For ever piping songs for ever new;
More happy love! more happy, happy love!
    For ever warm and still to be enjoy'd,
      For ever panting and for ever young;
All breathing human passion far above,
    That leaves a heart high-sorrowful and cloy'd,
      A burning forehead, and a parching tongue.

IV

Who are these coming to the sacrifice?
  To what green altar, O mysterious priest,
Lead'st thou that heifer lowing at the skies,
  And all her silken flanks with garlands drest?
What little town by river or sea-shore,
  Or mountain-built with peaceful citadel,
    Is emptied of its folk, this pious morn?
And, little town, thy streets for evermore
  Will silent be; and not a soul to tell
    Why thou art desolate can e'er return.

V

O Attic shape! Fair attitude! with brede
  Of marble men and maidens overwrought,
With forest branches and the trodden weed;
  Thou, silent form, dost tease us out of thought
As doth eternity: Cold Pastoral!
  When old age shall this generation waste,
    Thou shalt remain, in midst of other woe
Than ours, a friend to man, to whom thou say'st,
  'Beauty is truth, truth beauty,'—that is all
    Ye know on earth, and all ye need to know.

Ode to a nightingale

- brother died of TB
- depressed mood
- subjective
 then

I

My heart aches, and a drowsy numbness pains
  My sense, as though of hemlock I had drunk,
Or emptied some dull opiate to the drains
  One minute past, and Lethe-wards had sunk:
river of forgetfulness
'Tis not through envy of thy happy lot,
  But being too happy in thine happiness,—
    That thou, light-winged Dryad of the trees,
      In some melodious plot
Of beechen green, and shadows numberless,
  Singest of summer in full-throated ease.

42

II

O, for a draught of vintage! that hath been
  Cool'd a long age in the deep-delved earth,
Tasting of Flora and the country green,
  Dance, and Provençal song, and sunburnt mirth!
O for a beaker full of the warm South,
  Full of the true, the blushful Hippocrene,
    With beaded bubbles winking at the brim,
      And purple-stained mouth;
  That I might drink, and leave the world unseen,
    And with thee fade away into the forest dim:

III

Fade far away, dissolve, and quite forget
  What thou among the leaves hast never known,
The weariness, the fever, and the fret
  Here, where men sit and hear each other groan;
Where palsy shakes a few, sad, last gray hairs,
  Where youth grows pale, and spectre-thin, and dies;
    Where but to think is to be full of sorrow
      And leaden-eyed despairs,
  Where Beauty cannot keep her lustrous eyes,
    Or new Love pine at them beyond to-morrow.

IV

Away! away! for I will fly to thee,
  Not charioted by Bacchus and his pards,
But on the viewless wings of Poesy,
  Though the dull brain perplexes and retards:
Already with thee! tender is the night,
  And haply the Queen-Moon is on her throne,
    Cluster'd around by all her starry Fays;
      But here there is no light,
  Save what from heaven is with the breezes blown
    Through verdurous glooms and winding mossy ways.

V

I cannot see what flowers are at my feet,
  Nor what soft incense hangs upon the boughs,

But, in embalmed darkness, guess each sweet
 Wherewith the seasonable month endows
The grass, the thicket, and the fruit-tree wild;
 White hawthorn, and the pastoral eglantine;
  Fast fading violets cover'd up in leaves;
   And mid-May's eldest child,
 The coming musk-rose, full of dewy wine,
  The murmurous haunt of flies on summer eves.

VI

Darkling I listen; and, for many a time
 I have been half in love with easeful Death,
Call'd him soft names in many a mused rhyme,
 To take into the air my quiet breath;
Now more than ever seems it rich to die,
 To cease upon the midnight with no pain,
  While thou art pouring forth thy soul abroad
   In such an ecstasy!
 Still wouldst thou sing, and I have ears in vain—
  To thy high requiem become a sod.

VII

Thou wast not born for death, immortal Bird!
 No hungry generations tread thee down;
The voice I hear this passing night was heard
 In ancient days by emperor and clown:
Perhaps the self-same song that found a path
 Through the sad heart of Ruth, when, sick for home,
  She stood in tears amid the alien corn;
   The same that oft-times hath
 Charm'd magic casements, opening on the foam
  Of perilous seas, in faery lands forlorn.

VIII

Forlorn! the very word is like a bell
 To toll me back from thee to my sole self!
Adieu! the fancy cannot cheat so well
 As she is fam'd to do, deceiving elf.
Adieu! adieu! thy plaintive anthem fades
 Past the near meadows, over the still stream,

Up the hill-side; and now 'tis buried deep
   In the next valley-glades:
Was it a vision, or a waking dream?
   Fled is that music:—Do I wake or sleep?

When I have fears that I may cease to be

JOHN KEATS

When I have fears that I may cease to be
   Before my pen has glean'd my teeming brain,
Before high-piled books, in charactery,
   Hold like rich garners the full ripen'd grain;
When I behold, upon the night's starr'd face,
   Huge cloudy symbols of a high romance,
And think that I may never live to trace
   Their shadows, with the magic hand of chance;
And when I feel, fair creature of an hour,
   That I shall never look upon thee more,
Never have relish in the faery power
   Of unreflecting love;—then on the shore
Of the wide world I stand alone, and think
Till love and fame to nothingness do sink.

Ulysses

ALFRED, LORD TENNYSON

It little profits that an idle king,
By this still hearth, among these barren crags,
Match'd with an aged wife, I mete and dole
Unequal laws unto a savage race,
That hoard, and sleep, and feed, and know not me.
I cannot rest from travel: I will drink
Life to the lees: all times I have enjoy'd
Greatly, have suffer'd greatly, both with those
That loved me, and alone; on shore, and when
Thro' scudding drifts the rainy Hyades
Vext the dim sea: I am become a name;
For always roaming with a hungry heart

Much have I seen and known; cities of men
And manners, climates, councils, governments,
Myself not least, but honour'd of them all;
And drunk delight of battle with my peers,
Far on the ringing plains of windy Troy.
I am a part of all that I have met;
Yet all experience is an arch wherethro'
Gleams that untravell'd world, whose margin fades
For ever and for ever when I move.
How dull it is to pause, to make an end,
To rust unburnish'd, not to shine in use!
As tho' to breathe were life. Life piled on life
Were all too little, and of one to me
Little remains: but every hour is saved
From that eternal silence, something more,
A bringer of new things; and vile it were
For some three suns to store and hoard myself,
And this grey spirit yearning in desire
To follow knowledge like a sinking star,
Beyond the utmost bound of human thought.
    This is my son, mine own Telemachus,
To whom I leave the sceptre and the isle—
Well-loved of me, discerning to fulfil
This labour,. by slow prudence to make mild
A rugged people, and thro' soft degrees
Subdue them to the useful and the good.
Most blameless is he, centred in the sphere
Of common duties, decent not to fail
In offices of tenderness, and pay
Meet adoration to my household gods,
When I am gone. He works his work, I mine.
    There lies the port: the vessel puffs her sail:
There gloom the dark broad seas. My mariners,
Souls that have toil'd, and wrought, and thought with me—
That ever with a frolic welcome took
The thunder and the sunshine, and opposed
Free hearts, free foreheads—you and I are old;
Old age hath yet his honour and his toil;
Death closes all: but something ere the end,
Some work of noble note may yet be done,

Duke — 1st → aristocrat
2nd — connoisseur of beauty
3rd → lover & husband
cold, harsh, ruthless, hypocrite, sly

Not unbecoming men that strove with Gods.
The lights begin to twinkle from the rocks:
The long day wanes: the slow moon climbs: the deep
Moans round with many voices. Come, my friends,
'Tis not too late to seek a newer world.
Push off, and sitting well in order smite
The sounding furrows; for my purpose holds
To sail beyond the sunset, and the baths
Of all the western stars, until I die.
It may be that the gulfs will wash us down:
It may be we shall touch the Happy Isles,
And see the great Achilles, whom we knew.
Tho' much is taken, much abides; and tho'
We are not now that strength which in old days
Moved earth and heaven; that which we are, we are;
One equal temper of heroic hearts,
Made weak by time and fate, but strong in will
To strive, to seek, to find, and not to yield.

→ mini tragedy
→ 2 characters clearly developed

→ last wife 1) killed 2) nunnery 3) dungeon
→ Iambic Pentameter Rhyming Couplet

My last duchess → Dramatic monologue → Browning is a master
Set in Italy → 1846 → Browning eloped with Elizabeth Barret to It

ROBERT BROWNING

FERRARA

That's my last Duchess painted on the wall,
Looking as if she were alive. I call
That piece a wonder, now: Frà Pandolf's hands
Worked busily a day, and there she stands.
Will't please you sit and look at her? I said
'Frà Pandolf' by design, for never read
Strangers like you that pictured countenance,
The depth and passion of its earnest glance,
But to myself they turned (since none puts by
The curtain I have drawn for you, but I)
And seemed as they would ask me, if they durst,
How such a glance came there; so, not the first
Are you to turn and ask thus. Sir, 'twas not
Her husband's presence only, called that spot
Of joy into the Duchess' cheek: perhaps
Frà Pandolf chanced to say 'Her mantle laps

→ flattering her, too presumptuous

47

→ Appears nonchalant to subtly conveying threat
→ Study of evil and how power corrupt

Over my lady's wrist too much', or 'paint
Must never hope to reproduce the faint
Half-flush that dies along her throat': such stuff
Was courtesy, she thought, and cause enough
For calling up that spot of joy. She had
A heart . . . how shall I say?—too soon made glad,
Too easily impressed; she liked whate'er
She looked on, and her looks went everywhere.
Sir, 'twas all one! My favour at her breast,
The dropping of the daylight in the West,
The bough of cherries some officious fool
Broke in the orchard for her, the white mule
She rode with round the terrace—all and each
Would draw from her alike the approving speech,
Or blush, at least. She thanked men,—good! but thanked . . .
Somehow—I know not how—as if she ranked
My gift of a nine-hundred-years-old name
With anybody's gift. Who'd stoop to blame
This sort of trifling? Even had you skill
In speech—(which I have not)—to make your will
Quite clear to such an one, and say, 'Just this
Or that in you disgusts me; here you miss,
Or there exceed the mark'—and if she let
Herself be lessoned so, nor plainly set
Her wits to yours, forsooth, and made excuse,
—E'en then would be some stooping; and I choose
Never to stoop. Oh sir, she smiled, no doubt,
Whene'er I passed her; but who passed without
Much the same smile? This grew; I gave commands;
Then all smiles stopped together. There she stands
As if alive. Will't please you rise? We'll meet
The company below, then. I repeat,
The Count your master's known munificence
Is ample warrant that no just pretence
Of mine for dowry will be disallowed;
Though his fair daughter's self, as I avowed
At starting, is my object. Nay, we'll go
Together down, sir. Notice Neptune, though,
Taming a sea-horse, thought a rarity,
Which Claus of Innsbruck cast in bronze for me!

48

—Duke → can't appreciate simple, natural things
→ Natural rhythm → rhyme yet still colloquial appearance

The laboratory

ROBERT BROWNING

ANCIEN RÉGIME

I

Now that I, tying thy glass mask tightly,
May gaze thro' these faint smokes curling whitely,
As thou pliest thy trade in this devil's-smithy—
Which is the poison to poison her, prithee?

II

He is with her, and they know that I know
Where they are, what they do: they believe my tears flow
While they laugh, laugh at me, at me fled to the drear
Empty church, to pray God in, for them!—I am here.

III

Grind away, moisten and mash up thy paste,
Pound at thy powder,—I am not in haste!
Better sit thus, and observe thy strange things,
Than go where men wait me and dance at the King's.

IV

That in the mortar—you call it a gum?
Ah, the brave tree whence such gold oozings come!
And yonder soft phial, the exquisite blue,
Sure to taste sweetly,—is that poison too?

V

Had I but all of them, thee and thy treasures,
What a wild crowd of invisible pleasures!
To carry pure death in an earring, a casket,
A signet, a fan-mount, a filigree basket!

VI

Soon, at the King's a mere lozenge to give,
And Pauline should have just thirty minutes to live!
But to light a pastile, and Elise, with her head
And her breast and her arms and her hands, should drop dead!

VII

Quick—is it finished? The colour's too grim!
Why not soft like the phial's, enticing and dim?
Let it brighten her drink, let her turn it and stir,
And try it and taste, ere she fix and prefer!

VIII

What a drop! She's not little, no minion like me!
That's why she ensnared him: this never will free
The soul from those masculine eyes,—say, 'no!'
To that pulse's magnificent come-and-go.

IX

For only last night, as they whispered, I brought
My own eyes to bear on her so, that I thought
Could I keep them one half minute fixed, she would fall
Shrivelled; she fell not; yet this does it all!

X

Not that I bid you spare her the pain;
Let death be felt and the proof remain:
Brand, burn up, bite into its grace—
He is sure to remember her dying face!

XI

Is it done? Take my mask off! Nay, be not morose;
It kills her, and this prevents seeing it close:
The delicate droplet, my whole fortune's fee!
If it hurts her, beside, can it ever hurt me?

XII

Now, take all my jewels, gorge gold to your fill,
You may kiss me, old man, on my mouth if you will!
But brush this dust off me, lest horror it brings
Ere I know it—next moment I dance at the King's!

Prospice

Fear death?—to feel the fog in my throat,
　The mist in my face,
When the snows begin, and the blasts denote
　I am nearing the place,
The power of the night, the press of the storm,
　The post of the foe;
Where he stands, the Arch Fear in a visible form,
　Yet the strong man must go:
For the journey is done and the summit attained,
　And the barriers fall,
Though a battle's to fight e'er the guerdon be gained,
　The reward of it all.
I was ever a fighter, so—one fight more,
　The best and the last!
I would hate that death bandaged my eyes, and forebore,
　And bade me creep past.
No! let me taste the whole of it, fare like my peers
　The heroes of old,
Bear the brunt, in a minute pay glad life's arrears
　Of pain, darkness and cold.
For sudden the worst turns the best to the brave,
　The black minute's at end,
And the elements' rage, the fiend-voices that rave,
　Shall dwindle, shall blend,
Shall change, shall become first a peace out of pain,
　Then a light, then thy breast,
O thou soul of my soul! I shall clasp thee again,
　And with God be the rest!

Dover Beach

The sea is calm to-night.
The tide is full, the moon lies fair
Upon the straits;—on the French coast the light
Gleams and is gone; the cliffs of England stand,

Glimmering and vast, out in the tranquil bay.
Come to the window, sweet is the night-air!
Only, from the long line of spray
Where the sea meets the moon-blanch'd land,
Listen! you hear the grating roar
Of pebbles which the waves draw back, and fling,
At their return, up the high strand,
Begin, and cease, and then again begin,
With tremulous cadence slow, and bring
The eternal note of sadness in.

Sophocles long ago
Heard it on the Aegean, and it brought
Into his mind the turbid ebb and flow
Of human misery; we
Find also in the sound a thought,
Hearing it by this distant northern sea.

The Sea of Faith
Was once, too, at the full, and round earth's shore
Lay like the folds of a bright girdle furl'd.
But now I only hear
Its melancholy, long, withdrawing roar,
Retreating, to the breath
Of the night-wind, down the vast edges drear
And naked shingles of the world.

Ah, love let us be true
To one another! for the world, which seems
To lie before us like a land of dreams,
So various, so beautiful, so new,
Hath really neither joy, nor love, nor light,
Nor certitude, nor peace, nor help for pain;
And we are here as on a darkling plain
Swept with confused alarms of struggle and flight,
Where ignorant armies clash by night.

In time of 'the breaking of nations'

THOMAS HARDY

Only a man harrowing clods
  In a slow silent walk
With an old horse that stumbles and nods
  Half asleep as they stalk.

Only thin smoke without flame
  From the heaps of couch-grass;
Yet this will go onward the same
  Though Dynasties pass.

Yonder a maid and her wight
  Come whispering by;
War's annals will cloud into night
  Ere their story die.

God's grandeur

GERARD MANLEY HOPKINS

The world is charged with the grandeur of God.
  It will flame out, like shining from shook foil;
  It gathers to a greatness, like the ooze of oil
Crushed. Why do men then now not reck his rod?
Generations have trod, have trod, have trod;
  And all is seared with trade; bleared, smeared with toil;
  And wears man's smudge and shares man's smell: the soil!
Is bare now, nor can foot feel, being shod.

And for all this, nature is never spent;
  There lives the dearest freshness deep down things;
And though the last lights off the black West went
  Oh, morning, at the brown brink eastward, springs—
Because the Holy Ghost over the bent
  World broods with warm breast and with ah! bright wings.

Inversnaid

GERARD MANLEY HOPKINS

This darksome burn, horseback brown,
His rollrock highroad roaring down,
In coop and in comb the fleece of his foam
Flutes and low to the lake falls home.

A windpuff-bonnet of fáwn-fróth
Turns and twindles over the broth
Of a pool so pitchblack, féll-fró́wning,
It rounds and rounds Despair to drowning.

Degged with dew, dappled with dew
Are the groins of the braes that the brook threads through,
Wiry heathpacks, flitches of fern,
And the beadbonny ash that sits over the burn.

What would the world be, once bereft
Of wet and of wildness? Let them be left,
O let them be left, wildness and wet;
Long live the weeds and the wilderness yet.

Carrion comfort

GERARD MANLEY HOPKINS

Not, I'll not, carrion comfort, Despair, not feast on thee;
Not untwist—slack they may be—these last strands of man
In me ór, most weary, cry *I can no more.* I can;
Can something, hope, wish day come, not choose not to be.

But ah, but O thou terrible, why wouldst thou rude on me
Thy wring-world right foot rock? lay a lionlimb against me? scan
With darksome devouring eyes my bruisèd bones? and fan,
O in turns of tempest, me heaped there; me frantic to avoid thee and
    flee?

Why? That my chaff might fly; my grain lie, sheer and clear.
Nay in all that toil, that coil, since (seems) I kissed the rod,

Hand rather, my heart lo! lapped strength, stole joy, would laugh, chéer.

Cheer whom though? The hero whose heaven-handling flung me, fóot tród
Me? or me that fought him? O which one? is it each one? That night, that year
Of now done darkness I wretch lay wrestling with (my God!) my God.

My own heart let me have more pity on

GERARD MANLEY HOPKINS

My own heart let me have more pity on; let
Me live to my sad self hereafter kind,
Charitable; not live this tormented mind
With this tormented mind tormenting yet.

I cast for comfort I can no more get
By groping round my comfortless, than blind
Eyes in their dark can day or thirst can find
Thirst's all-in-all in all a world of wet.

Soul, self; come, poor Jackself, I do advise
You, jaded, let be; call off thoughts awhile
Elsewhere; leave comfort root-room; let joy size

At God knows when to God knows what; whose smile
's not wrung, see you; unforeseen times rather—as skies
Betweenpie mountains—lights a lovely mile.

THEME: Problem of man's inability to understand the ways of God (ie. good people suffer)

Thou art indeed just, Lord, if I contend with thee

GERARD MANLEY HOPKINS (1844-1889)

Thou art indeed just, Lord, if I contend
With thee; but, sir, so what I plead is just.
Why do sinners' ways prosper? and why must
Disappointment all I endeavour end?

55

Wert thou my enemy, O thou my friend,
How wouldst thou worse, I wonder, than thou dost
Defeat, thwart me? Oh, the sots and thralls of lust
Do in spare hours more thrive than I that spend,

Sir, life upon thy cause. See, banks and brakes
Now, leavèd how thick! lacèd they are again
With fretty chervil, look, and fresh wind shakes
Them; birds build—but not I build; no, but strain,
Time's eunuch, and not breed one work that wakes.
Mine, O thou lord of life, send my roots rain.

Eight o'clock

A. E. HOUSMAN

He stood, and heard the steeple
    Sprinkle the quarters on the morning town.
One, two, three, four, to market-place and people
    It tossed them down.

Strapped, noosed, nighing his hour,
    He stood and counted them and cursed his luck;
And then the clock collected in the tower
    Its strength, and struck.

The wild swans at Coole

WILLIAM BUTLER YEATS

The trees are in their autumn beauty,
The woodland paths are dry,
Under the October twilight the water
Mirrors a still sky;
Upon the brimming water among the stones
Are nine-and-fifty swans.

56

[Handwritten annotations at top:] IRONY: SWANS SEEM TO CHANGE MORE IN THAN POEM → IRONY ⌐1st → merely probs be later powerful symbols

[Right margin handwritten:] ⓢ speed, suddenness ⓑ he can do nothing about it

The nineteenth autumn has come upon me
Since I first made my count; *→ was there 19 years ago*
I saw, before I had well finished, *→ didn't have time to finish → slow, old*
All suddenly mount *→ sex connotations*
And scatter wheeling in great broken rings *→ Natural cycle of the swans → immortal → wedding ring*
Upon their clamorous wings. *→ broken — regret he couldn't marry his beloved* *mortal immortal*

I have looked upon those brilliant creatures, *→ he is not brilliant* *loudness of wings → projection of his own heart cunly*
And now my heart is sore. *← to be able to partake pleasure of life* *realises that death is near — why*
All's changed since I, hearing at twilight, *→ again*
The first time on this shore, *← when he was young, virile, passionate*
The bell-beat of their wings above my head, *vital, quicker beat*
Trod with a lighter tread. *lighter rhythm → youth*

Unwearied still, lover by lover, *← swans seem to resist defeat & ravages of time & he is even* *swans are in pairs & he is alone → CONTRAST*
They paddle in the cold *quiet, unmoving yet*
Companionable streams or climb the air; *i.e. birds have companions* *PARADOX: man is not at home in cold water* *immortality* } *at home in both environments*
Their hearts have not grown old; *← has love & life/restless* *earth: mortality*
Passion or conquest, wander where they will, *← envy's them → immortal span & limited to park*
Attend upon them still. *personified as royal servants* *kneeling upon them → noble / regal birds*

But now they drift on the still water, *→ at home in all elements*
Mysterious, beautiful; *comes to term with aging/death by knowledge that the beautiful*
Among what rushes will they build, *& the fly away } swans will always be there to delight men*
By what lake's edge or pool
Delight men's eyes when I awake some day *→ acceptance — a positive note who will enjoy their*
To find they have flown away? *→ literal → referring to death → awake → flown beauty after they have away* *→ or awake to harsh reality no longer here*

→ Romantic obsession with time/death → repeated thru

PASSION → FIRE } CONQUEST — ICE

- Better to live short, exciting life than long boring inspired by death of Lady Gregory's one *son in WWI (pilot in air)* *- non-sentimental, honest view → sincerity*

An Irish airman foresees his death

- Great figure in Irish theatre
WILLIAM BUTLER YEATS → [1865-1939]
- Patron = Lady Gregory
- Symbolic, religious ideas
- Abt → Nobel Prize

Narrator = Irishman → attributes to flying → I, personal statement → Flies for fun, not war

I know that I shall meet my fate *A death in the clouds*
Somewhere among the clouds above; *a swan's destiny*
Those that I fight I do not hate, *German — any conventional excuse*
Those that I guard I do not love; *British — honest*
My country is Kiltartan Cross, *Freedom County*
My countrymen Kiltartan's poor, *love for Ireland*
No likely end could bring them loss *attitude to the war — Irish people*
Or leave them happier than before. *again rejects conventional reasons for fighting in war*

57

[Bottom handwritten:] Iambic tetrameter 4 regular quatrains

Nor law, nor duty bade me fight,
Nor public men, nor cheering crowds,
A lonely impulse of delight
Drove to this tumult in the clouds;
I balanced all, brought all to mind,
The years to come seemed waste of breath,
A waste of breath the years behind
In balance with this life, this death.

The second coming

Turning and turning in the widening gyre
The falcon cannot hear the falconer;
Things fall apart; the centre cannot hold;
Mere anarchy is loosed upon the world,
The blood-dimmed tide is loosed, and everywhere
The ceremony of innocence is drowned;
The best lack all conviction, while the worst
Are full of passionate intensity.

Surely some revelation is at hand;
Surely the Second Coming is at hand.
The Second Coming! Hardly are those words out
When a vast image out of *Spiritus Mundi*
Troubles my sight: somewhere in sands of the desert
A shape with lion body and the head of a man,
A gaze blank and pitiless as the sun,
Is moving its slow thighs, while all about it
Reel shadows of the indignant desert birds.
The darkness drops again; but now I know
That twenty centuries of stony sleep
Were vexed to nightmare by a rocking cradle,
And what rough beast, its hour come round at last,
Slouches towards Bethlehem to be born?

History

LAURENCE BINYON

Time has stored all, but keeps his chronicle
In secret, beyond all our probe or gauge.
There flows the human story, vast and full;
And here a muddy trickle smears the page.

The things our hearts remember make a sound
So faint; so loud the menace and applause.
The gleaners come, with eyes upon the ground
After Oblivion's harvest, picking straws.

What is man, if this only has told his tale,
For whom ruin and blunder mark the years,
Whom continent-shadowing conquerors regale
To surfeiting, with glory of blood and tears?

He flaunts his folly and woe in a proud dress:
But writes no history of his happiness.

Mending wall

ROBERT FROST

Something there is that doesn't love a wall,
That sends the frozen-ground-swell under it,
And spills the upper boulders in the sun;
And makes gaps even two can pass abreast.
The work of hunters is another thing:
I have come after them and made repair
Where they have left not one stone on a stone,
But they would have the rabbit out of hiding,
To please the yelping dogs. The gaps I mean,
No one has seen them made or heard them made,
But at spring mending-time we find them there.
I let my neighbour know beyond the hill;
And on a day we meet to walk the line
And set the wall between us once again.
We keep the wall between us as we go.
To each the boulders that have fallen to each.

And some are loaves and some so nearly balls
We have to use a spell to make them balance:
'Stay where you are until our backs are turned!'
We wear our fingers rough with handling them.
Oh, just another kind of outdoor game,
One on a side. It comes to little more:
There where it is we do not need the wall:
He is all pine and I am apple orchard.
My apple trees will never get across
And eat the cones under his pines, I tell him.
He only says, 'Good fences make good neighbours.'
Spring is the mischief in me, and I wonder
If I could put a notion in his head:
'*Why* do they make good neighbours? Isn't it
Where there are cows? But here there are no cows.
Before I built a wall I'd ask to know
What I was walling in or walling out,
And to whom I was like to give offence.
Something there is that doesn't love a wall,
That wants it down.' I could say 'Elves' to him,
But it's not elves exactly, and I'd rather
He said it for himself. I see him there
Bringing a stone grasped firmly by the top
In each hand, like an old-stone savage armed.
He moves in darkness as it seems to me,
Not of woods only and the shade of trees.
He will not go behind his father's saying,
And he likes having thought of it so well
He says again, 'Good fences make good neighbours.'

After apple-picking

ROBERT FROST

My long two-pointed ladder's sticking through a tree
Toward heaven still,
And there's a barrel that I didn't fill
Beside it, and there may be two or three
Apples I didn't pick upon some bough.
But I am done with apple-picking now.

Essence of winter sleep is on the night,
The scent of apples: I am drowsing off.
I cannot rub the strangeness from my sight
I got from looking through a pane of glass
I skimmed this morning from the drinking trough
And held against the world of hoary grass.
It melted, and I let it fall and break.
But I was well
Upon my way to sleep before it fell,
And I could tell
What form my dreaming was about to take.
Magnified apples appear and disappear,
Stem end and blossom end,
And every fleck of russet showing clear.
My instep arch not only keeps the ache,
It keeps the pressure of a ladder-round.
I feel the ladder sway as the boughs bend.
And I keep hearing from the cellar bin
The rumbling sound
Of load on load of apples coming in.
For I have had too much
Of apple-picking: I am overtired
Of the great harvest I myself desired.
There were ten thousand thousand fruit to touch,
Cherish in hand, lift down, and not let fall.
For all
That struck the earth,
No matter if not bruised or spiked with stubble,
Went sure to the cider-apple heap
As of no worth.
One can see what will trouble
This sleep of mine, whatever sleep it is.
Were he not gone,
The woodchuck could say whether it's like his
Long sleep, as I describe its coming on,
Or just some human sleep.

Birches

ROBERT FROST

When I see birches bend to left and right
Across the lines of straighter darker trees,
I like to think some boy's been swinging them.
But swinging doesn't bend them down to stay
As ice-storms do. Often you must have seen them
Loaded with ice a sunny winter morning
After a rain. They click upon themselves
As the breeze rises, and turn many-coloured
As the stir cracks and crazes their enamel.
Soon the sun's warmth makes them shed crystal shells
Shattering and avalanching on the snow-crust—
Such heaps of broken glass to sweep away
You'd think the inner dome of heaven had fallen.
They are dragged to the withered bracken by the load,
And they seem not to break; though once they are bowed
So low for long, they never right themselves:
You may see their trunks arching in the woods
Years afterwards, trailing their leaves on the ground
Like girls on hands and knees that throw their hair
Before them over their heads to dry in the sun.
But I was going to say when Truth broke in
With all her matter-of-fact about the ice-storm
I should prefer to have some boy bend them
As he went out and in to fetch the cows—
Some boy too far from town to learn baseball,
Whose only play was what he found himself,
Summer or winter, and could play alone.
One by one he subdued his father's trees
By riding them down over and over again
Until he took the stiffness out of them,
And not one but hung limp, not one was left
For him to conquer. He learned all there was
To learn about not launching out too soon
And so not carrying the tree away
Clear to the ground. He always kept his poise
To the top branches, climbing carefully
With the same pains you use to fill a cup

Up to the brim, and even above the brim.
Then he flung outward, feet first, with a swish,
Kicking his way down through the air to the ground.
So was I once myself a swinger of birches.
And so I dream of going back to be.
It's when I'm weary of considerations,
And life is too much like a pathless wood
Where your face burns and tickles with the cobwebs
Broken across it, and one eye is weeping
From a twig's having lashed across it open.
I'd like to get away from earth awhile
And then come back to it and begin over.
May no fate wilfully misunderstand me
And half grant what I wish and snatch me away
Not to return. Earth's the right place for love:
I don't know where it's likely to go better.
I'd like to go by climbing a birch tree,
And climb black branches up a snow-white trunk
Toward heaven, till the tree could bear no more,
But dipped its top and set me down again.
That would be good both going and coming back.
One could do worse than be a swinger of birches.

Stopping by woods on a snowy evening

ROBERT FROST

Whose woods these are I think I know.
His house is in the village though;
He will not see me stopping here
To watch his woods fill up with snow.

My little horse must think it queer
To stop without a farmhouse near
Between the woods and frozen lake
The darkest evening of the year.

He gives his harness bells a shake
To ask if there is some mistake.
The only other sound's the sweep
Of easy wind and downy flake.

The woods are lovely, dark and deep,
But I have promises to keep,
And miles to go before I sleep,
And miles to go before I sleep.

Snake

D. H. LAWRENCE

A snake came to my water-trough
On a hot, hot day, and I in pyjamas for the heat,
To drink there.

In the deep, strange-scented shade of the great dark carob-tree
I came down the steps with my pitcher
And must wait, must stand and wait, for there he was at the trough
    before me.

He reached down from a fissure in the earth-wall in the gloom
And trailed his yellow-brown slackness soft-bellied down, over the edge
    of the stone trough
And rested his throat upon the stone bottom,
And where the water had dripped from the tap, in a small clearness,
He sipped with his straight mouth,
Softly drank through his straight gums, into his slack long body,
Silently.

Someone was before me at my water-trough,
And I, like a second comer, waiting.

He lifted his head from his drinking, as cattle do,
And looked at me vaguely, as drinking cattle do,
And flickered his two-forked tongue from his lips, and mused a
    moment,
And stooped and drank a little more,
Being earth-brown, earth-golden from the burning bowels of the earth
On the day of Sicilian July, with Etna smoking.

The voice of my education said to me
He must be killed,
For in Sicily the black, black snakes are innocent, the gold are
    venomous.

64

And voices in me said, If you were a man
You would take a stick and break him now, and finish him off.

But must I confess how I liked him,
How glad I was he had come like a guest in quiet, to drink at my water
    trough
And depart peaceful, pacified, and thankless,
Into the burning bowels of this earth?

Was it cowardice, that I dared not kill him?
Was it perversity, that I longed to talk to him?
Was it humility, to feel so honoured?
I felt so honoured.

And yet those voices:
If you were not afraid, you would kill him!

And truly I was afraid, I was most afraid,
But even so, honoured still more
That he should seek my hospitality
From out the dark door of the secret earth.

He drank enough
And lifted his head, dreamily, as one who has drunken,
And flickered his tongue like a forked night on the air, so black;
Seeming to lick his lips,
And looked around like a god, unseeing, into the air,
And slowly turned his head,
And slowly, very slowly, as if thrice adream,
Proceeded to draw his slow length curving round
And climb again the broken bank of my wall-face.

And as he put his head into that dreadful hole,
And as he slowly drew up, snake-easing his shoulders, and entered
    farther,
A sort of horror, a sort of protest against his withdrawing into that
    horrid black hole,
Deliberately going into the blackness and slowly drawing himself
    after,
Overcame me now his back was turned.

I looked round, I put down my pitcher,
I picked up a clumsy log
And threw it at the water-trough with a clatter.

I think it did not hit him,
But suddenly that part of him that was left behind convulsed in
    undignified haste,
Writhed like lightning, and was gone
Into the black hole, the earth-lipped fissure in the wall-front,
At which, in the intense still noon, I stared with fascination.

And immediately I regretted it.
I thought how paltry, how vulgar, what a mean act!
I despised myself and the voices of my accursed human education.

And I thought of the albatross,
And I wished he would come back, my snake.

For he seemed to me again like a king,
Like a king in exile, uncrowned in the underworld,
Now due to be crowned again.

And so, I missed my chance with one of the lords
Of life.
And I have something to expiate;
A pettiness.

Bat —emotive - subjective — not factual/literal & imaginative

D. H. LAWRENCE

At evening, sitting on this terrace,
When the sun from the west, beyond Pisa, beyond the mountains of
    Carrara
Departs, and the world is taken by surprise . . .

When the tired flower of Florence is in gloom beneath the glowing
Brown hills surrounding . . .

When under the arches of the Ponte Vecchio
A green light enters against stream, flush from the west,
Against the current of obscure Arno . . .

Look up, and you see things flying
Between the day and the night;
Swallows with spools of dark thread sewing the shadows together.

A circle swoop, and a quick parabola under the bridge arches
Where light pushes through;
A sudden turning upon itself of a thing in the air.
A dip to the water.

And you think:
'The swallows are flying so late!'

Swallows?

Dark air-life looping
Yet missing the pure loop . . .
A twitch, a twitter, an elastic shudder in flight
And serrated wings against the sky,
Like a glove, a black glove thrown up at the light,
And falling back.

Never swallows!
Bats!
The swallows are gone.

At a wavering instant the swallows give way to bats
By the Ponte Vecchio . . .
Changing guard.

Bats, and an uneasy creeping in one's scalp
As the bats swoop overhead!
Flying madly.

Pipistrello!
Black piper on an infinitesimal pipe.
Little lumps that fly in air and have voices indefinite, wildly vindictive!

Wings like bits of umbrella.

Bats!

Creatures that hang themselves up like an old rag, to sleep;
And disgustingly upside down.
Hanging upside down like rows of disgusting old rags
And grinning in their sleep.
Bats!

In China the bat is symbol of happiness.

Not for me!

Mountain lion

D. H. LAWRENCE

Climbing through the January snow, into the Lobo Canyon
Dark grow the spruce trees, blue is the balsam, water sounds still
    unfrozen, and the trail is still evident.

Men!
Two men!
Men! The only animal in the world to fear!

They hesitate.
We hesitate.
They have a gun.
We have no gun.

Then we all advance, to meet.

Two Mexicans, strangers, emerging out of the dark and snow and
    inwardness of the Lobo valley.
What are they doing here on this vanishing trail?

What is he carrying?
Something yellow.
A deer?

Qué tiene, amigo?
Léon—

He smiles, foolishly, as if he were caught doing wrong.
And we smile, foolishly, as if we didn't know.
He is quite gentle and dark-faced.

It is a mountain lion,
A long, long slim cat, yellow like a lioness.
Dead.

He trapped her this morning, he says, smiling foolishly.

Lift up her face,
Her round, bright face, bright as frost.
Her round, fine-fashioned head, with two dead ears;
And stripes in the brilliant frost of her face, sharp, fine dark rays,
Dark, keen, fine rays in the brilliant frost of her face.
Beautiful dead eyes.

Hermoso es!

They go out towards the open;
We go on into the gloom of Lobo.
And above the trees I found her lair,
A hole in the blood-orange brilliant rocks that stick up, a little cave.
And bones, and twigs, and a perilous ascent.

So she will never leap up that way again, with the yellow flash of a
    mountain lion's long shoot!
And her bright striped frost-face will never watch any more, out of
    the shadow of the cave in the blood-orange rock,
Above the trees of the Lobo dark valley-mouth!

Instead I look out.
And out to the dim of the desert, like a dream, never real;
To the snow of the Sangre de Cristo mountains, the ice of the
    mountains of Picoris,
And near across at the opposite steep of snow, green trees motionless
    standing in snow, like a Christmas toy.

And I think in this empty world there was room for me and a mountain
    lion.
And I think in the world beyond, how easily we might spare a million
    or two of humans
And never miss them.
Yet what a gap in the world, the missing white frost-face of that slim
    yellow mountain lion!

Heaven

RUPERT BROOKE

Fish (fly-replete, in depth of June,
Dawdling away their wat'ry noon)
Ponder deep wisdom, dark or clear,
Each secret fishy hope or fear.
Fish say, they have their Stream and Pond;
But is there anything Beyond?
This life cannot be All, they swear,
For how unpleasant, if it were!

One may not doubt that, somehow, Good
Shall come of Water and of Mud;
And, sure, the reverent eye must see
A Purpose in Liquidity.
We darkly know, by Faith we cry,
The future is not Wholly Dry.
Mud unto mud!—Death eddies near—
Not here the appointed End, not here!
But somewhere, beyond Space and Time,
Is wetter water, slimier slime!
And there (they trust) there swimmeth One
Who swam ere rivers were begun,
Immense, of fishy form and mind,
Squamous, omnipotent, and kind;
And under that Almighty Fin,
The littlest fish may enter in.
Oh! never fly conceals a hook,
Fish say, in the Eternal Brook,
But more than mundane weeds are there,
And mud, celestially fair;
Fat caterpillars drift around,
And Paradisal grubs are found;
Unfading moths, immortal flies,
And the worm that never dies.
And in that Heaven of all their wish,
There shall be no more land, say fish.

The hill

(1888-1915)
RUPERT BROOKE

Breathless, we flung us on the windy hill,
    Laughed in the sun, and kissed the lovely grass.
    You said, 'Through glory and ecstasy we pass;
Wind, sun, and earth remain, the birds sing still,
When we are old, are old. . . .' 'And when we die
    All's over that is ours; and life burns on
Through other lovers, other lips,' said I,
    'Heart of my heart, our heaven is now, is won!'

'We are Earth's best, that learnt her lesson here.
   Life is our cry. We have kept the faith!' we said;
   'We shall go down with unreluctant tread
Rose-crowned into the darkness!' . . . Proud we were,
And laughed, that had such brave true things to say.
—And then you suddenly cried, and turned away.

→ no regular rhythym, line length, free verse
→ drabness / squalour / frustration of life in t modern city
→ dreary modern life → meaningless life
c. 1910

Preludes *→ musical introduction*
& Ironic: it is a prelude to *(1888–1965)* nothing **T. S. ELIOT**
→ I–III introduce a different time of day
→ no clear, logical exposition →
→ suggestive poet → builds on sequences
→ sordid, objective, laconic (few words) of images
→ Religious man - direct
Society to greater
spirituality
→ life meaningless w/o fai
→ reflects aridity of indus
→ rhythym is ironic

I

The winter evening settles down
With smell of steaks in passageways. *→ slum tenants*
Six o'clock. *→ rigid mechanical* *→ conformity → everyone cooking steak*
The burnt-out ends of smoky days. *→ cigarette image - smokes*
And now a gusty shower wraps *→ pollution - lack of anything fresh/new*
The grimy scraps *→ rain → should be refreshing & not in the city*
→ dirty *→ no rich/abundant life*
Of withered leaves about your feet
And newspapers from vacant lots; *by wind*
The showers beat *→ strong word - pain/hostility*
On broken blinds and chimney-pots, *→ broken contacts - no real link*
→ poverty/neglected
And at the corner of the street
A lonely cab-horse steams and stamps.
And then the lighting of the lamps. *→ not natural - rigid - not natural day*

II
→ traditionally reflected/pure
The morning comes to consciousness *→ memory of the past*
Of faint stale smells of beer *→ hangover / waste / loss*
From the sawdust-trampled street *→ put down to cover... spit tarred roads*
With all its muddy feet that press *→ lack of privacy - large numbers of people*
To early coffee-stands. *→ modern/artificial convenience*
With the other masquerades *→ always acting - unreality - lack of personality*
That time resumes, *→ taken up again in t morning*
One thinks of all the hands
That are raising dingy shades *→ monotony, sameness -*
In a thousand furnished rooms. *→ depersonalisation - boredom / horror*
→ no personal contact

71

III

You tossed a blanket from the bed,
You lay upon your back, and waited;
You dozed, and watched the night revealing
The thousand sordid images
Of which your soul was constituted;
They flickered against the ceiling.
And when all the world came back
And the light crept up between the shutters
And you heard the sparrows in the gutters,
You had such a vision of the street
As the street hardly understands;
Sitting along the bed's edge, where
You curled the papers from your hair,
Or clasped the yellow soles of feet
In the palms of both soiled hands.

IV

His soul stretched tight across the skies
That fade behind a city block,
Or trampled by insistent feet
At four and five and six o'clock;
And short square fingers stuffing pipes,
And evening newspapers, and eyes
Assured of certain certainties,
The conscience of a blackened street
Impatient to assume the world.

I am moved by fancies that are curled
Around these images, and cling:
The notion of some infinitely gentle
Infinitely suffering thing.

Wipe your hand across your mouth, and laugh;
The worlds revolve like ancient women
Gathering fuel in vacant lots.

72

Journey of the Magi

T. S. ELIOT

'A cold coming we had of it,
Just the worst time of the year
For a journey, and such a long journey:
The ways deep and the weather sharp,
The very dead of winter.'
And the camels galled, sore-footed, refractory,
Lying down in the melting snow.
There were times we regretted
The summer palaces on slopes, the terraces,
And the silken girls bringing sherbet.
Then the camel men cursing and grumbling
And running away, and wanting their liquor and women,
And the night-fires going out, and the lack of shelters,
And the cities hostile, and the towns unfriendly
And the villages dirty and charging high prices:
A hard time we had of it.
At the end we preferred to travel all night,
Sleeping in snatches,
With the voices singing in our ears, saying
That this was all folly.

    Then at dawn we came down to a temperate valley,
Wet, below the snow line, smelling of vegetation;
With a running stream and a water-mill beating the darkness,
And three trees on the low sky,
And an old white horse galloped away in the meadow.
Then we came to a tavern with vine-leaves over the lintel,
Six hands at an open door dicing for pieces of silver,
And feet kicking the empty wine-skins.
But there was no information, and so we continued
And arrived at evening, not a moment too soon
Finding the place; it was (you may say) satisfactory.

    All this was a long time ago, I remember,
And I would do it again, but set down
This set down
This: were we led all that way for
Birth or Death? There was a Birth, certainly,

We had evidence and no doubt. I had seen birth and death,
But had thought they were different; this Birth was
Hard and bitter agony for us, like Death, our death.
We returned to our places, these Kingdoms,
But no longer at ease here, in the old dispensation,
With an alien people clutching their gods.
I should be glad of another death.

Triumphal march

T. S. ELIOT

Stone, bronze, stone, steel, stone, oakleaves, horses' heels
Over the paving.
And the flags. And the trumpets. And so many eagles.
How many? Count them. And such a press of people.
We hardly knew ourselves that day, or knew the City.
This is the way to the temple, and we so many crowding the way.
So many waiting, how many waiting? what did it matter, on such a
    day?
Are they coming? No, not yet. You can see some eagles. And hear
    the trumpets.
Here they come. Is he coming?
The natural wakeful life of our Ego is a perceiving.
We can wait with our stools and our sausages.
What comes first? Can you see? Tell us. It is

        5,800,000 rifles and carbines,
          102,000 machine guns,
           28,000 trench mortars,
           53,000 field and heavy guns,
I cannot tell how many projectiles, mines and fuses.
           13,000 aeroplanes,
           24,000 aeroplane engines,
           50,000 ammunition waggons,
now   55,000 army waggons,
           11,000 field kitchens,
            1,150 field bakeries.

What a time that took. Will it be he now? No,
Those are the golf club Captains, these the Scouts,

And now the *société gymnastique de Poissy*
And now come the Mayor and the Liverymen. Look
There he is now, look:
There is no interrogation in his eyes
Or in the hands, quiet over the horse's neck,
And the eyes watchful, waiting, perceiving, indifferent.
O hidden under the dove's wing, hidden in the turtle's breast,
Under the palmtree at noon, under the running water
At the still point of the turning world. O hidden.

Now they go up to the temple. Then the sacrifice.
Now come the virgins bearing urns, urns containing
Dust
Dust
Dust of dust, and now
Stone, bronze, stone, steel, stone, oakleaves, horses' heels
Over the paving.

That is all we could see. But how many eagles! and how many
    trumpets!
(And Easter Day, we didn't get to the country,
So we took young Cyril to church. And they rang a bell
And he said right out loud, *crumpets*.)
                          Don't throw away that sausage,
It'll come in handy. He's artful. Please, will you
Give us a light?
Light
Light
Et les soldats faisaient la haie? ILS LA FAISAIENT.

Greater love

WILFRED OWEN

Red lips are not so red
  As the stained stones kissed by the English dead.
Kindness of wooed and wooer
Seems shame to their love pure.
O Love, your eyes lose lure
  When I behold eyes blinded in my stead!

Your slender attitude
  Trembles not exquisite like limbs knife-skewed,
Rolling and rolling there
Where God seems not to care;
Till the fierce love they bear
  Cramps them in death's extreme decrepitude.

Your voice sings not so soft,—
  Though even as wind murmuring through raftered loft,—
Your dear voice is not dear,
Gentle, and evening clear,
As theirs whom none now hear,
  Now earth has stopped their piteous mouths that coughed.

Heart, you were never hot,
  Nor large, nor full like hearts made great with shot;
And though your hand be pale,
Paler are all which trail
Your cross through flame and hail:
  Weep, you may weep, for you may touch them not.

poem - satire/exposé of war - reveals horror
poet - bitter, angry, pity for those who died

Dulce et decorum est

sweet   suitable   it is
*   proper*
*bitterly
ironic -*

WILFRED OWEN

undignified
exhausted   not heroicly portrayed
Bent double, like old beggars under sacks,—*all → difficult to pronounce*
They are "under weight   old witches + what way → should be tall, virile
weary Knock-kneed, coughing like hags, we cursed through sludge,—*smelted snow/mud*
flames, fires of battle   →poet knows what it's like
lit + fire Till on the haunting flares we turned our backs
light haunting   euphemism 4 death
fear, strain of And towards our distant rest began to trudge.
battle haunt →   so tired   mud sucked them off feet - blood covers feet
image of battle Men marched asleep. Many had lost their boots,
will remain with But limped on, blood-shod. All went lame; all blind;—*in some way they have*
them   war dehumanizes   all suffer
feel failing over as if drunk but lit from exhaustion
Drunk with fatigue; deaf even to the hoots—*gas shells - onomatopoeia*
Of tired, outstripped Five-Nines that dropped behind.
↳ so tired that they hear 2 late

*   comradeire, closeness, youth*
activity Gas! GAS! Quick, boys!—An ecstasy of fumbling,
urgency, fear, blind panic conveyed -   diff. types of typography
Fitting the clumsy helmets just in time;—*in fear, calmes clif to fasten*
'ecstasy' But someone still was yelling out and stumbling—*burning his legs, eyes*
= frenzy
f. - all it And floundr'ing like a man in fire or lime. . . .
takes a long
time to put   **76**   *Liquid sound as tho he is gassed*
on masks   *Drowning in water & lime burns*

Dim, through the misty panes and thick green light, *- of fumes*

As under a green sea, I saw him drowning. *choking*

as assaulted by nightmare *when awake - can suppress into subconscious*

- horrible, slow, agonising death

In all my dreams, before my helpless sight, *-> similie sustained - helpless in sleep*

He plunges at me, guttering, choking, drowning. *red. going out like candle* *fear rises to surface & torments him*

- shows *painful death*

g it *-> fears smothered in helpless nightmares*

ags If in some smothering dreams you too could pace *- what he has seen*

like a carcass

Behind the wagon that we flung him in, *war dehumanizes, no time for anyth. else*

assonance *twisting*

And watch the white eyes writhing in his face, *head hanging over side of wager*

hows His hanging face, like a devil's sick of sin; *- suffering didn't look human - ghastly excess*

arn *of death -> image of sin / corruption -*

ike If you could hear, at every jolt, the blood *bitter senses, powerful images* *images regurgitated*

bursting acid

ged man Come gargling from the froth-corrupted lungs, *enjamb*

Obscene as cancer, bitter as the cud *was regular war sickness, corruption* *met 2 show lies* } *anti-war attitude, sickness, corruption of society morals*

en a claw *sickness repetiton of innocent boys' Last lie* Of vile, incurable sores on innocent tongues,—

ud *If you only you could experiencing what *

hb sfied My friend, you would not tell with such high zest

To children ardent for some desperate glory, *-every time they want 2 go 2 war*

emphasized falseness

The old Lie: Dulce et decorum est *- shows devastion of WWI, suffering*

Pro patria mori. *- dismisses it as a brief le* *vision of reality*

4 it's country 2 die

- Latin gives it impressive dignity

-tragic loss of life, inhuman slaughter

distinguished by half-rhyme (para rhyme) & assonance

↳shows cacophony, clamour, harshness (not perfect rhyme)

-'zest'- naeve enthusiasm | poem - unified, irony emphasized honest representation of futility of war - not under haze of romantic patriotism

Anthem for doomed youth

WILFRED OWEN

What passing bells for these who die as cattle?
    Only the monstrous anger of the guns.
    Only the stuttering rifles' rapid rattle
Can patter out their hasty orisons.
No mockeries now; for them no prayers nor bells,
    Nor any voice of mourning save the choirs,—
The shrill, demented choirs of wailing shells;
    And bugles calling for them from sad shires.

What candles may be held to speed them all?
    Not in the hands of boys, but in their eyes
Shall shine the holy glimmers of good-byes.
    The pallor of girls' brows shall be their pall;
Their flowers the tenderness of patient minds,
And each slow dusk a drawing-down of blinds.

Strange meeting

WILFRED OWEN

It seemed that out of battle I escaped
Down some profound dull tunnel, long since scooped
Through granites which titanic wars had groined.
Yet also there encumbered sleepers groaned,
Too fast in thought or death to be bestirred.
Then, as I probed them, one sprang up, and stared
With piteous recognition in fixed eyes,
Lifting distressful hands as if to bless.
And by his smile, I knew that sullen hall,
By his dead smile I knew we stood in Hell.
With a thousand pains that vision's face was grained;
Yet no blood reached there from the upper ground,
And no guns thumped, or down the flues made moan.
'Strange friend,' I said, 'here is no cause to mourn.'
'None,' said that other, 'save the undone years,
The hopelessness. Whatever hope is yours,
Was my life also; I went hunting wild
After the wildest beauty in the world,
Which lies not calm in eyes, or braided hair,
But mocks the steady running of the hour,
And if it grieves, grieves richlier than here.
For of my glee might many men have laughed,
And of my weeping something had been left,
Which must die now. I mean the truth untold,
The pity of war, the pity war distilled.
Now men will go content with what we spoiled.
Or, discontent, boil bloody, and be spilled.
They will be swift with swiftness of the tigress,
None will break ranks, though nations trek from progress.
Courage was mine, and I had mystery,
Wisdom was mine, and I had mastery;
To miss the march of this retreating world
Into vain citadels that are not walled.
Then, when much blood had clogged their chariot-wheels
I would go up and wash them from sweet wells,
Even with truths that lie too deep for taint.
I would have poured my spirit without stint

But not through wounds; not on the cess of war.
Foreheads of men have bled where no wounds were.
I am the enemy you killed, my friend.
I knew you in this dark: for so you frowned
Yesterday through me as you jabbed and killed.
I parried; but my hands were loath and cold.
Let us sleep now. . . .'

anyone lived in a pretty how town

e. e. cummings

anyone lived in a pretty how town
(with up so floating many bells down)
spring summer autumn winter
he sang his didn't he danced his did.

Women and men (both little and small)
cared for anyone not at all
they sowed their isn't they reaped their same
sun moon stars rain

children guessed (but only a few
and down they forgot as up they grew
autumn winter spring summer)
that noone loved him more by more

when by now and tree by leaf
she laughed his joy she cried his grief
bird by snow and stir by still
anyone's any was all to her

someones married their everyones
laughed their cryings and did their dance
(sleep wake hope and then) they
said their nevers and slept their dream

stars rain sun moon
(and only the snow can begin to explain
how children are apt to forget to remember
with up so floating many bells down)

79

one day anyone died i guess
(and noone stooped to kiss his face)
busy folk buried them side by side
little by little and was by was

all by all and deep by deep
and more by more they dream their sleep
noone and anyone earth by april
wish by spirit and if by yes.

Women and men (both dong and ding)
summer autumn winter spring
reaped their sowing and went their came
sun moon stars rain

what if a much of a which of a wind

e. e. cummings

what if a much of a which of a wind
gives the truth to summer's lie;
bloodies with dizzying leaves the sun
and yanks immortal stars awry?
Blow king to beggar and queen to seem
(blow friend to fiend:blow space to time)
—when skies are hanged and oceans drowned,
the single secret will still be man

what if a keen of a lean wind flays
screaming hills with sleet and snow:
strangles valleys by ropes of thing
and stifles forests in white ago?
Blow hope to terror;blow seeing to blind
(blow pity to envy and soul to mind)
—whose hearts are mountains,roots are trees,
it's they shall cry hello to the spring

what if a dawn of a doom of a dream
bites this universe in two,
peels forever out of his grave
and sprinkles nowhere with me and you?

80

Blow soon to never and never to twice
(blow life to isn't:blow death to was)
—all nothing's only our hugest home;
the most who die,the more we live

somewhere i have never travelled

somewhere i have never travelled,gladly beyond
any experience,your eyes have their silence:
in your most frail gesture are things which enclose me,
or which i cannot touch because they are too near

your slightest look easily will unclose me
though i have closed myself as fingers,
you open always petal by petal myself as Spring opens
(touching skilfully,mysteriously) her first rose

or if your wish be to close me,i and
my life will shut very beautifully,suddenly,
as when the heart of this flower imagines
the snow carefully everywhere descending;

nothing which we are to perceive in this world equals
the power of your intense fragility:whose texture
compels me with the colour of its countries,
rendering death and forever with each breathing

(i do not know what it is about you that closes
and opens;only something in me understands
the voice of your eyes is deeper than all roses)
nobody,not even the rain,has such small hands

The cool web

Children are dumb to say how hot the day is,
How hot the scent is of the summer rose,
How dreadful the black wastes of evening sky,
How dreadful the tall soldiers drumming by.

But we have speech, to chill the angry day,
And speech, to dull the rose's cruel scent.
We spell away the overhanging night,
We spell away the soldiers and the fright.

There's a cool web of language winds us in,
Retreat from too much joy or too much fear:
We grow sea-green at last and coldly die
In brininess and volubility.

But if we let our tongues lose self-possession,
Throwing off language and its watery clasp
Before our death, instead of when death comes,
Facing the wide glare of the children's day,
Facing the rose, the dark sky and the drums
We shall go mad no doubt and die that way.

The serf

ROY CAMPBELL

His naked skin clothed in the torrid mist
That puffs in smoke around the patient hooves,
The ploughman drives, a slow somnambulist,
And through the green his crimson furrow grooves.
His heart, more deeply than he wounds the plain,
Long by the rasping share of insult torn,
Red clod, to which the war-cry once was rain
And tribal spears the fatal sheaves of corn,
Lies fallow now. But as the turf divides
I see in the slow progress of his strides
Over the toppled clods and falling flowers,
The timeless, surly patience of the serf
That moves the nearest to the naked earth
And ploughs down palaces, and thrones, and towers.

The Zulu girl

When in the sun the hot red acres smoulder,
Down where the sweating gang its labour plies,
A girl flings down her hoe, and from her shoulder
Unslings her child tormented by the flies.

She takes him to a ring of shadow pooled
By thorn-trees: purpled with the blood of ticks,
While her sharp nails, in slow caresses ruled,
Prowl through his hair with sharp electric clicks.

His sleepy mouth, plugged by the heavy nipple,
Tugs like a puppy, grunting as he feeds:
Through his frail nerves her own deep langours ripple
Like a broad river sighing through its reeds.

Yet in that drowsy stream his flesh imbibes
An old unquenched unsmotherable heat—
The curbed ferocity of beaten tribes,
The sullen dignity of their defeat.

Her body looms above him like a hill
Within whose shade a village lies at rest,
Or the first cloud so terrible and still
That bears the coming harvest in its breast.

Horses on the Camargue

In the grey wastes of dread,
The haunt of shattered gulls where nothing moves
But in a shroud of silence like the dead,
I heard a sudden harmony of hooves,
And, turning, saw afar
A hundred snowy horses unconfined,
The silver runaways of Neptune's car
Racing, spray-curled, like waves before the wind.

Sons of the Mistral, fleet
As him with whose strong gusts they love to flee,
Who shod the flying thunders on their feet
And plumed them with the snortings of the sea;
Theirs is no earthly breed
Who only haunt the verges of the earth
And only on the sea's salt herbage feed—
Surely the great white breakers gave them birth.
For when for years a slave,
A horse of the Camargue, in alien lands,
Should catch some far-off fragrance of the wave
Carried far inland from his native sands,
Many have told the tale
Of how in fury, foaming at the rein,
He hurls his rider; and with lifted tail,
With coal-red eyes and cataracting mane,
Heading his course for home,
Though sixty foreign leagues before him sweep,
Will never rest until he breathes the foam
And hears the native thunder of the deep.
But when the great gusts rise
And lash their anger on these arid coasts,
When the scared gulls career with mournful cries
And whirl across the wastes like driven ghosts:
When hail and fire converge,
The only souls to which they strike no pain
Are the white-crested fillies of the surge
And the white horses of the windy plain.
Then in their strength and pride
The stallions of the wilderness rejoice;
They feel their Master's trident in their side,
And high and shrill they answer to his voice.
With white tails smoking free,
Long streaming manes and arching necks, they show
Their kinship to their sisters of the sea—
And forward hurl their thunderbolts of snow.
Still out of hardship bred,
Spirits of power and beauty and delight
Have ever on such frugal pastures fed
And loved to course with tempests through the night.

84

Tristan da Cunha

ROY CAMPBELL

Snore in the foam; the night is vast and blind;
The blanket of the mist about your shoulders,
Sleep your old sleep of rock, snore in the wind,
Snore in the spray! the storm your slumber lulls,
His wings are folded on your nest of boulders
As on their eggs the grey wings of your gulls.

No more as when, so dark an age ago,
You hissed a giant cinder from the ocean,
Around your rocks you furl the shawling snow
Half sunk in your own darkness, vast and grim,
And round you on the deep with surly motion
Pivot your league-long shadow as you swim.

Why should you haunt me thus but that I know
My surly heart is in your own displayed,
Round whom such leagues in endless circuit flow,
Whose hours in such a gloomy compass run—
A dial with its league-long arm of shade
Slowly revolving to the moon and sun.

My pride has sunk, like your grey fissured crags,
By its own strength o'ertoppled and betrayed:
I, too, have burned the wind with fiery flags
Who now am but a roost for empty words,
An island of the sea whose only trade
Is in the voyages of its wandering birds.

Did you not, when your strength became your pyre,
Deposed and tumbled from your flaming tower,
Awake in gloom from whence you sank in fire,
To find, Antaeus-like, more vastly grown,
A throne in your own darkness, and a power
Sheathed in the very coldness of your stone?

Your strength is that you have no hope or fear,
You march before the world without a crown,
The nations call you back, you do not hear,
The cities of the earth grow grey behind you,

You will be there when their great flames go down
And still the morning in the van will find you.

You march before the continents, you scout
In front of all the earth; alone you scale
The mast-head of the world, a lorn look-out,
Waving the snowy flutter of your spray
And gazing back in infinite farewell
To suns that sink and shores that fade away.

From your grey tower what long regrets you fling
To where, along the low horizon burning,
The great swan-breasted seraphs soar and sing,
And suns go down, and trailing splendours dwindle,
And sails on lonely errands unreturning
Glow with a gold no sunrise can rekindle.

Turn to the night; these flames are not for you
Whose steeple for the thunder swings its bells;
Grey Memnon, to the tempest only true,
Turn to the night, turn to the shadowing foam,
And let your voice, the saddest of farewells,
With sullen curfew toll the grey wings home.

The wind, your mournful syren, haunts the gloom;
The rocks, spray-clouded, are your signal guns
Whose stony nitre, puffed with flying spume,
Rolls forth in grim salute your broadside hollow
Over the gorgeous burials of suns
To sound the tocsin of the storms that follow.

Plunge forward like a ship to battle hurled,
Slip the long cables of the failing light,
The level rays that moor you to the world:
Sheathed in your armour of eternal frost,
Plunge forward, in the thunder of the fight
To lose yourself as I would fain be lost.

Exiled like you and severed from my race
By the cold ocean of my own disdain,
Do I not freeze in such a wintry space,
Do I not travel through a storm as vast

And rise at times, victorious from the main,
To fly the sunrise at my shattered mast?

Your path is but a desert where you reap
Only the bitter knowledge of your soul:
You fish with nets of seaweed in the deep
As fruitlessly as I with nets of rhyme—
Yet forth you stride, yourself the way, the goal,
The surges are your strides, your path is time.

Hurled by what aim to what tremendous range!
A missile from the great sling of the past,
Your passage leaves its track of death and change
And ruin on the world: you fly beyond
Leaping the current of the ages vast
As lightly as a pebble skims a pond.

The years are undulations in your flight
Whose awful motion we can only guess—
Too swift for sense, too terrible for sight,
We only know how fast behind you darken
Our days like lonely beacons of distress:
We know that you stride on and will not harken.

Now in the eastern sky the fairest planet
Pierces the dying wave with dangled spear,
And in the whirling hollows of your granite
That vaster sea to which you are a shell
Sighs with a ghostly rumour, like the drear
Moan of the nightwind in a hollow cell.

We shall not meet again; over the wave
Our ways divide, and yours is straight and endless,
But mine is short and crooked to the grave:
Yet what of these dark crowds amid whose flows
I battle like a rock, aloof and friendless,
Are not their generations vague and endless
The waves, the strides, the feet on which I go?

Come live with me and be my love

C. DAY LEWIS

Come live with me and be my love,
And we will all the pleasures prove
Of peace and plenty, bed and board,
That chance employment may afford.

I'll handle dainties on the docks
And thou shalt read of summer frocks:
At evening by the sour canals
We'll hope to hear some madrigals.

Care on thy maiden brow shall put
A wreath of wrinkles, and thy foot
Be shod with pain: not silken dress
But toil shall tire thy loveliness.

Hunger shall make thy modest zone
And cheat fond death of all but bone—
If these delights thy mind may move,
Then live with me and be my love.

Let us now praise famous men

C. DAY LEWIS

Let us now praise famous men,
Not your earth-shakers, not the dynamiters,
But who in the Home Counties or the Khyber,
Trimming their sails to meet an ill wind,
Facing the Adversary with a clean collar,
Justified the system.
Admire the venerable pile that bred them,
Bones are its foundations,
The pinnacles are stone abstractions,
Whose halls are whispering-galleries designed
To echo voices of the past, dead tongues.
White hopes of England here
Are taught to rule by learning to obey.

Bend over before vested interests,
Kiss the rod, salute the quarter-deck;
Here is no savage discipline
Of peregrine swooping, of fire destroying,
But a civil code; no capital offender
But the cool cad, the man who goes too far.
Ours the curriculum
Neither of building birds nor wasteful waters,
Bound in books not violent in vein:
Here we inoculate with dead ideas
Against blood-epidemics, against
The infection of faith and the excess of life.
Our methods are up to date; we teach
Through head and not by heart,
Language with gramophones and sex with charts,
Prophecy by deduction, prayer by numbers.
For honours see prospectus: those who leave us
Will get a post and pity the poor;
Their eyes glaze at strangeness;
They are never embarrassed, have a word for everything,
Living on credit, dying when the heart stops;
Will wear black armlets and stand a moment in silence
For the passing of an era, at their own funeral.

A time to dance

For those who had the power
    of the forest fires that burn
Leaving their source in ashes
    to flush the sky with fire:
Those whom a famous urn
    could not contain, whose passion
Brimmed over the deep grave
    and dazzled epitaphs:
For all that have won us wings
    to clear the tops of grief,
My friend who within me laughs
    bids you dance and sing.

Some set out to explore
   earth's limit, and little they recked if
Never their feet came near it
   outgrowing the need for glory:
Some aimed at a small objective
   but the fierce updraught of their spirit
Forced them to the stars.
   Are honoured in public who built
The dam that tamed a river;
   or holding the salient for hours
Against odds, cut off and killed,
   are remembered by one survivor.

All these. But most for those
   whom accident made great,
As a radiant chance encounter
   of cloud and sunlight grows
Immortal on the heart:
   whose gift was the sudden bounty
Of a passing moment, enriches
   the fulfilled eye for ever.
Their spirits rose serene
   above time's roughest reaches,
But their seed is in us and over
   our lives they are evergreen.

Look, stranger

W. H. AUDEN

Look, stranger, on this island now
The leaping light for your delight discovers,
Stand stable here
And silent be,
That through the channels of the ear
May wander like a river
The swaying sound of the sea.

Here at the small field's ending pause
Where the chalk wall falls to the foam, and its tall ledges
Oppose the pluck

And knock of the tide,
And the shingle scrambles after the sucking surf,
And the gull lodges
A moment on its sheer side.

Far off like floating seeds the ships
Diverge on urgent voluntary errands;
And the full view
Indeed may enter
And move in memory as now these clouds do,
That pass the harbour mirror
And all the summer through the water saunter.

Musée des Beaux Arts

About suffering they were never wrong,
The Old Masters: how well they understood
Its human position; how it takes place
While someone else is eating or opening a window or just walking dully
	along;
How, when the aged are reverently, passionately waiting
For the miraculous birth, there always must be
Children who do not specially want it to happen, skating
On a pond at the edge of the wood:
They never forgot
That even the dreadful martyrdom must run its course
Anyhow in a corner, some untidy spot
Where the dogs go on with their doggy life and the torturer's horse
Scratches its innocent behind on a tree.

In Brueghel's *Icarus*, for instance: how everything turns away
Quite leisurely from the disaster; the ploughman may
Have heard the splash, the forsaken cry,
But for him it was not an important failure; the sun shone
As it had to on the white legs disappearing into the green
Water; and the expensive delicate ship that must have seen
Something amazing, a boy falling out of the sky,
Had somewhere to get to and sailed calmly on.

The unknown citizen

W. H. AUDEN

TO

JS/07/M/378

THIS MARBLE MONUMENT IS ERECTED

BY THE STATE

He was found by the Bureau of Statistics to be
One against whom there was no official complaint,
And all the reports of his conduct agree
That, in the modern sense of an old-fashioned word, he was a saint,
For in everything he did he served the Greater Community.
Except for the War till the day he retired
He worked in a factory and never got fired,
But satisfied his employers, Fudge Motors Inc.
Yet he wasn't a scab or odd in his views,
For his Union reports that he paid his dues,
(Our report on his Union shows it was sound)
And our Social Psychology workers found
That he was popular with his mates and liked a drink.
The Press are convinced that he bought a paper every day
And that his reactions to advertisements were normal in every way.
Policies taken out in his name prove that he was fully insured,
And his Health-card shows he was once in hospital but left it cured.
Both Producers Research and High-Grade Living declare
He was fully sensible to the advantages of the Instalment Plan
And he had everything necessary to the Modern Man,
A gramophone, a radio, a car and a frigidaire.
Our researchers into Public Opinion are content
That he held the proper opinions for the time of year;
When there was peace, he was for peace; when there was war, he went.
He was married and added five children to the population,
Which our Eugenist says was the right number for a parent of his
    generation,
And our teachers report that he never interfered with their education
Was he free? Was he happy? The question is absurd:
Had anything been wrong, we should certainly have heard.

Lay your sleeping head

W. H. AUDEN

Lay your sleeping head, my love,
Human on my faithless arm;
Time and fevers burn away
Individual beauty from
Thoughtful children, and the grave
Proves the child ephemeral:
But in my arms till break of day
Let the living creature lie,
Mortal, guilty, but to me
The entirely beautiful.

Soul and body have no bounds:
To lovers as they lie upon
Her tolerant enchanted slope
In their ordinary swoon,
Grave the vision Venus sends
Of supernatural sympathy,
Universal love and hope;
While an abstract insight wakes
Among the glaciers and the rocks
The hermit's carnal ecstasy.

Certainty, fidelity
On the stroke of midnight pass
Like vibrations of a bell,
And fashionable madmen raise
Their pedantic boring cry:
Every farthing of the cost,
All the dreaded cards foretell,
Shall be paid, but from this night
Not a whisper, not a thought,
Not a kiss nor look be lost.

Beauty, midnight, vision dies:
Let the winds of dawn that blow
Softly round your dreaming head
Such a day of sweetness show

Eye and knocking heart may bless,
Find our mortal world enough;
Noons of dryness find you fed
By the involuntary powers,
Nights of insult let you pass
Watched by every human love.

Prayer before birth

LOUIS MACNEICE

I am not yet born; O hear me.
Let not the bloodsucking bat or the rat or the stoat or the club-
  footed ghoul come near me.

I am not yet born; console me.
I fear that the human race may with tall walls wall me,
  with strong drugs dope me, with wise lies lure me,
    on black racks rack me, in blood-baths roll me.

I am not yet born; provide me
With water to dandle me, grass to grow for me, trees to talk
  to me, sky to sing to me, birds and a white light
    in the back of my mind to guide me.

I am not yet born; forgive me
For the sins that in me the world shall commit, my words
  when they speak me, my thoughts when they think me,
    my treason engendered by traitors beyond me,
      my life when they murder by means of my
        hands, my death when they live me.

I am not yet born; rehearse me
In the parts I must play and the cues I must take when
  old men lecture me, bureaucrats hector me, mountains
    frown at me, lovers laugh at me, the white
      waves call me to folly and the desert calls
        me to doom and the beggar refuses
          my gift and my children curse me.

94

LABOUR PAINS

I am not yet born; O hear me,
Let not the man who is beast or who thinks he is God
  come near me.

I am not yet born; O fill me
With strength against those who would freeze my
  humanity, would dragoon me into a lethal automaton,
    would make me a cog in a machine, a thing with
      one face, a thing, and against all those
        who would dissipate my entirety, would
          blow me like thistledown hither and
            thither or hither and thither
              like water held in the
                hands would spill me.

Let them not make me a stone and let them not spill me.
Otherwise kill me.

Meeting point

LOUIS MACNEICE

Time was away and somewhere else
There were two glasses and two chairs
And two people with the one pulse
(Somebody stopped the moving stairs):
Time was away and somewhere else.

And they were neither up nor down
The stream's music did not stop
Flowing through heather, limpid brown,
Although they sat in a coffee shop
And they were neither up nor down.

The bell was silent in the air
Holding its inverted poise—
Between the clang and clang a flower,
A brazen calyx of no noise:
The bell was silent in the air.

95

— POWER OF LOVE

— Love/imagination creates rich world

The camels crossed the miles of sand — their imagination · table is an infinite space
That stretched around the cups and plates; — anti-climax — reality of world
The desert was their own, they planned — world belongs to them
To portion out the stars and dates: — they have the power/control/ability
The camels crossed the miles of sand. — desert - symbol of eternity — goal-like

Time S

Time was away and somewhere else. — real world contrasted with Love
The waiter did not come, the clock — they forgot time - dreamy/in love
Forgot them and the radio waltz — usual sights transform into music/beauty
Came out like water from a rock: — Biblical Image · magic
Time was away and somewhere else. — moment of perfect peace/unity

SPACE T

Her fingers flicked away the ash — She is smoking
That bloomed again in tropic trees: — re-birth — time inverted — everything heightened by love - rich/splendour
Not caring if the markets crash — business — does not affect them at all
When they had forests such as these,
Her fingers flicked away the ash.

Time S

God or whatever means the Good — whoever is responsible for love/such moment
Be praised that time can stop like this, — love - timeless
That what the heart has understood — in love - fulfilled, in harmony
Can verify in the body's peace — released - life is perfect
God or whatever means the Good. — constant repetition

SPACE T

Time was away and she was here — love presence creates radiance
And life no longer what it was, — he is also transformed ... of love
The bell was silent in the air — radiance of love
And all the room a glow because — tremendous power · regular rhyme/rhythm · lovers can create their own world
Time was away and she was here.

THEME: Transience of youth, life, love
— sad, beautiful lyric

The sunlight on the garden

LOUIS MACNEICE 1907–1963

— rhyme - dovetails the lines + gives impression of echo
— all joys last too long
— love, warmth, youth, hope

The sunlight on the garden — life, beauty, colourful appealing
Hardens and grows cold, — death → rigor mortis / childhood → age, grey
We cannot cage the minute — resigned tone - note bitterness
Within its nets of gold, — good & bad things are ephemeral
When all is told — good, wonderful, precious / told → counted money
We cannot beg for pardon — cannot remain on earth forever / excused

96

Our freedom as free lances
Advances towards its end;
The earth compels, upon it
Sonnets and birds descend;
And soon, my friend,
We shall have no time for dances.

The sky was good for flying
Defying the church bells
And every evil iron
Siren and what it tells:
The earth compels,
We are dying, Egypt, dying

And not expecting pardon,
Hardened in heart anew,
But glad to have sat under
Thunder and rain with you,
And grateful too
For sunlight on the garden.

An elementary school classroom in a slum

STEPHEN SPENDER

Far far from gusty waves these children's faces.
Like rootless weeds, the hair torn round their pallor.
The tall girl with her weighed-down head. The paper-
seeming boy, with rat's eyes. The stunted, unlucky heir
Of twisted bones, reciting a father's gnarled disease,
His lesson from his desk. At back of the dim class
One unnoted, sweet and young. His eyes live in a dream
Of squirrel's game, in tree room, other than this.

On sour cream walls, donations. Shakespeare's head,
Cloudless at dawn, civilized dome riding all cities.
Belled, flowery, Tyrolese valley. Open-handed map
Awarding the world its world. And yet, for these

Children, these windows, not this world, are world,
Where all their future's painted with a fog,
A narrow street sealed in with a lead sky,
Far far from rivers, capes, and stars of words.

Surely, Shakespeare is wicked, the map a bad example
With ships and sun and love tempting them to steal—
For lives that slyly turn in their cramped holes
From fog to endless night? On their slag heap, these children
Wear skins peeped through by bones and spectacles of steel
With mended glass, like bottle bits on stones.
All of their time and space are foggy slum.
So blot their maps with slums as big as doom.

Unless, governor, teacher, inspector, visitor,
This map becomes their window and these windows
That shut upon their lives like catacombs,
Break O break open till they break the town
And show the children to green fields and make their world
Run azure on gold sands, and let their tongues
Run naked into books, the white and green leaves open
History theirs whose language is the sun.

I think continually of those who were truly great

STEPHEN SPENDER

I think continually of those who were truly great.
Who, from the womb, remembered the soul's history
Through corridors of light where the hours are suns,
Endless and singing. Whose lovely ambition
Was that their lips, still touched with fire,
Should tell of the Spirit, clothed from head to foot in song.
And who hoarded from the Spring branches
The desires falling across their bodies like blossoms.

What is precious, is never to forget
The essential delight of the blood drawn from ageless springs
Breaking through rocks in worlds before our earth.
Never to deny its pleasure in the morning simple light

Nor its grave evening demand for love.
Never to allow gradually the traffic to smother
With noise and fog, the flowering of the Spirit.

Near the snow, near the sun, in the highest fields,
See how these names are fêted by the waving grass
And by the streamers of white cloud
And whispers of wind in the listening sky.
The names of those who in their lives fought for life,
Who wore at their hearts the fire's centre.
Born of the sun, they travelled a short while towards the sun
And left the vivid air signed with their honour.

And death shall have no dominion

DYLAN THOMAS

And death shall have no dominion.
Dead men naked they shall be one
With the man in the wind and the west moon;
When their bones are picked clean and the clean bones gone,
They shall have stars at elbow and foot;
Though they go mad they shall be sane,
Though they sink through the sea they shall rise again;
Though lovers be lost love shall not;
And death shall have no dominion.

And death shall have no dominion.
Under the windings of the sea
They lying long shall not die windily;
Twisting on racks when sinews give way,
Strapped to a wheel, yet they shall not break;
Faith in their hands shall snap in two,
And the unicorn evils run them through;
Split all ends up they shan't crack;
And death shall have no dominion.

And death shall have no dominion.
No more may gulls cry at their ears
Or waves break loud on the seashores;

Where blew a flower may a flower no more
Lift its head to the blows of the rain;
Though they be mad and dead as nails,
Heads of the characters hammer through daisies;
Break in the sun till the sun breaks down,
And death shall have no dominion.

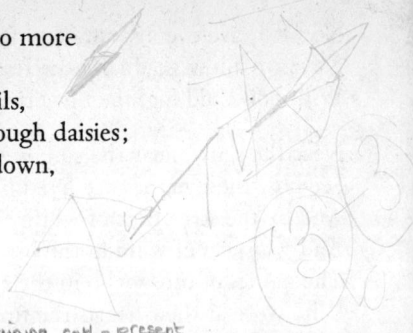

Poem in October

DYLAN THOMAS

It was my thirtieth year to heaven
Woke to my hearing from harbour and neighbour wood
And the mussel pooled and the heron
        Priested shore
    The morning beckon
With water praying and call of seagull and rook
And the knock of sailing boats on the net webbed wall
        Myself to set foot
            That second
In the still sleeping town and set forth.

My birthday began with the water-
Birds and the birds of the winged trees flying my name
Above the farms and the white horses
            And I rose
        In rainy autumn
And walked abroad in a shower of all my days.
High tide and the heron dived when I took the road
        Over the border
            And the gates
Of the town closed as the town awoke.

    A springful of larks in a rolling
Cloud and the roadside bushes brimming with whistling
    Blackbirds and the sun of October
            Summery
        On the hill's shoulder,
Here were fond climates and sweet singers suddenly

Come in the morning where I wandered and listened
    To the rain wringing
        Wind blow cold
    In the wood faraway under me.

    Pale rain over the dwindling harbour
And over the sea wet church the size of a snail
    With its horns through mist and the castle
        Brown as owls
        But all the gardens
Of spring and summer were blooming in the tall tales
Beyond the border and under the lark full cloud.
        There could I marvel
            My birthday
    Away but the weather turned around.

        It turned away from the blithe country
And down the other air and the blue altered sky
    Streamed again a wonder of summer
        With apples
        Pears and red currants
And I saw in the turning so clearly a child's
Forgotten mornings when he walked with his mother
    Through the parables
        Of sun light
    And the legends of the green chapels

    And the twice told fields of infancy
That his tears burned my cheeks and his heart moved in mine.
    These were the woods the river and sea
        Where a boy
        In the listening
Summertime of the dead whispered the truth of his joy
To the trees and the stones and the fish in the tide.
        And the mystery
            Sang alive
    Still in the water and singingbirds.

    And there could I marvel my birthday
Away but the weather turned around. And the true
    Joy of the long dead child sang burning
        In the sun.

101

(handwritten annotations in margins:)
→ Past gone & still in his heart
→ associated with → harmony → size of snail relative
spire
→ mother told him
→ he remembers
→ memories of youth
over
→ of time
→ retains childlike wonder → not cynical / disillusioned
gay, happy
→ warm on the hill
liquid
→ spring, youth
? → taste, nourishment, sustenance — lack of inhibition, energy
by remembers when
→ 3rd person
→ lessons from nature / sunlight
→ memories like film be screened again
that child
pr. past
feelings are like a child's
he (like boy) is in touch with mystery life
PARADOX
— At one with nature
1/14/1~
feels young again
person

It was my thirtieth
Year to heaven stood there then in the summer noon
Though the town below lay leaved with October blood.
O may my heart's truth
Still be sung
On this high hill in a year's turning.

The hunchback in the park

DYLAN THOMAS

The hunchback in the park
A solitary mister
Propped between trees and water
From the opening of the garden lock
That lets the trees and water enter
Until the Sunday sombre bell at dark

Eating bread from a newspaper
Drinking water from the chained cup
That the children filled with gravel
In the fountain basin where I sailed my ship
Slept at night in a dog kennel
But nobody chained him up.

Like the park birds he came early
Like the water he sat down
And Mister they called Hey mister
The truant boys from the town
Running when he had heard them clearly
On out of sound

Past lake and rockery
Laughing when he shook his paper
Hunchbacked in mockery
Through the loud zoo of the willow groves
Dodging the park keeper
With his stick that picked up leaves.

And the old dog sleeper
Alone between nurses and swans
While the boys among willows
Made the tigers jump out of their eyes
To roar on the rockery stones
And the groves were blue with sailors

Made all day until bell time
A woman figure without fault
Straight as a young elm
Straight and tall from his crooked bones
That she might stand in the night
After the locks and chains

All night in the unmade park
After the railings and shrubberies
The birds the grass the trees the lake
And the wild boys innocent as strawberries
Had followed the hunchback
To his kennel in the dark.

Do not go gentle into that good night

DYLAN THOMAS

Do not go gentle into that good night,
Old age should burn and rave at close of day;
Rage, rage against the dying of the light.

Though wise men at their end know dark is right,
Because their words had forked no lightning they
Do not go gentle into that good night.

Good men, the last wave by, crying how bright
Their frail deeds might have danced in a green bay,
Rage, rage against the dying of the light.

Wild men who caught and sang the sun in flight,
And learn, too late, they grieved it on its way,
Do not go gentle into that good night.

from - town child spending holiday on cousin's farm - natural if
adult eye, mind & heart begins to make presence felt
- contrasts A & C - absorbed, unburdened by past & future
burdened by past-quilt   - not inhibited in the now
apprehensive about future

Grave men, near death, who see with blinding sight
Blind eyes could blaze like meteors and be gay,
Rage, rage against the dying of the light.

And you, my father, there on the sad height,
Curse, bless, me now with your fierce tears, I pray.
Do not go gentle into that good night.
Rage, rage against the dying of the light.

Fern Hill

DYLAN THOMAS

Now as I was young and easy under the apple boughs
About the lilting house and happy as the grass was green,
   The night above the dingle starry,
     Time let me hail and climb
   Golden in the heydays of his eyes,
And honoured among wagons I was prince of the apple towns
And once below a time I lordly had the trees and leaves
     Trail with daisies and barley
   Down the rivers of the windfall light.

And as I was green and carefree, famous among the barns
About the happy yard and singing as the farm was home,
   In the sun that is young once only,
     Time let me play and be
   Golden in the mercy of his means,
And green and golden I was huntsman and herdsman, the calves
Sang to my horn, the foxes on the hills barked clear and cold,
     And the sabbath rang slowly
   In the pebbles of the holy streams.

All the sun long it was running, it was lovely, the hay
Fields high as the house, the tunes from the chimneys, it was air
   And playing, lovely and watery
   And fire green as grass.
   And nightly under the simple stars
As I rode to sleep the owls were bearing the farm away,
All the moon long I heard, blessed among stables, the nightjars
   Flying with the ricks, and the horses
   Flashing into the dark.

And then to awake, and the farm, like a wanderer white
With the dew, come back, the cock on his shoulder: it was all
   Shining, it was Adam and maiden,
      The sky gathered again
    And the sun grew round that very day.
So it must have been after the birth of the simple light
In the first, spinning place, the spellbound horses walking warm
     Out of the whinnying green stable
      On to the fields of praise.

And honoured among foxes and pheasants by the gay house
Under the new made clouds and happy as the heart was long,
   In the sun born over and over,
    I ran my heedless ways,
   My wishes raced through the house high hay
And nothing I cared, at my sky blue trades, that time allows
In all his tuneful turning so few and such morning songs
    Before the children green and golden
     Follow him out of grace,

Nothing I cared, in the lamb white days, that time would take me
Up to the swallow thronged loft by the shadow of my hand,
   In the moon that is always rising,
     Nor that riding to sleep
   I should hear him fly with the high fields
And wake to the farm forever fled from the childless land.
Oh I was young and easy in the mercy of his means,
    Time held me green and dying
   Though I sang in my chains like the sea.

Cape Coloured batman

GUY BUTLER

As the slanting sun drowsed lazily
On the terraced groves of Tuscany
At last I found him, back to a trunk:
Nelson, my batman, the bastard, drunk.

On the grass beneath an olive tree
His legs lay splayed in a khaki V
And all his body, relaxed, at ease,
Head thrown back, while over his knees
Strumming the banjo his yellow hands
Stirred all his sorrow from four steel strands.

His melancholy cries from Hollywood,
'Where the coyotes cry' or 'Lady be Good',
In that declining light awoke
A tenderness for the stupid bloke,
So happy his sorrow, so at ease
Strumming the strings across his knees.

No doubt a pirate Javanese
From Malacca Straits or Sunda Seas
Shaped those almond eyes of his;

A Negress from the Cameroons—
Bought for brandy, sold for doubloons—
Gave him a voice that wails and croons;

An eagle Arab trading far
From Hadramaut to Zanzibar
Left him a nose like a scimitar;

A Bush-girl from the Namaqua sands
Bequeathed him bird-like, restless hands
Stirring his sorrow from four steel strands;

While English, Dutch and Portuguese
Sick of biscuits and sodden cheese
Put in at the Tavern of the Seas,

Northerners warm in the Southern night
Drank red Cape brandy, and got tight—
And left him a skin that's almost white.

This is the man the Empires made
From lesser breeds, the child of Trade
Left without hope in History's shade;

Shouldered aside into any old place,
Damned from birth by the great disgrace,
A touch of the tar-brush in his face.

Under pines, mimosas and mango trees
Strewn through the world lie men like these:
Drunk crooning voices, banjos on knees.

He fell asleep in a vinous mist,
Star in his mouth, bottle in fist,
The desperate, maudlin hedonist.

But the pathos of the human race
Sainted his drunken, relaxed face;
And a warm dusk wind through the olive trees
Touched mute strings across his knees
With sorrows from the Seven Seas.

Hawk roosting

TED HUGHES

I sit in the top of the wood, my eyes closed.
Inaction, no falsifying dream
Between my hooked head and my hooked feet:
Or in sleep rehearse perfect kills and eat.

The convenience of the high trees!
The air's buoyancy and the sun's ray
Are of advantage to me;
And the earth's face upward for my inspection.

My feet are locked upon the rough bark.
It took the whole of Creation
To produce my foot, my each feather:
Now I hold Creation in my foot

Or fly up, and revolve it all slowly—
I kill where I please because it is all mine.
There is no sophistry in my body:
My manners are tearing off heads—

The allotment of death.
For the one path of my flight is direct
Through the bones of the living.
No arguments assert my right:

The sun is behind me.
Nothing has changed since I began.
My eye has permitted no change.
I am going to keep things like this.

The horses

TED HUGHES

I climbed through woods in the hour-before-dawn dark.
Evil air, a frost-making stillness,

Not a leaf, not a bird,—
A world cast in frost. I came out above the wood

Where my breath left tortuous statues in the iron light.
But the valleys were draining the darkness

Till the moorline—blackening dregs of the brightening grey—
Halved the sky ahead. And I saw the horses:

Huge in the dense grey—ten together—
Megalith-still. They breathed, making no move,

With draped manes and tilted hind-hooves,
Making no sound.

I passed: not one snorted or jerked its head.
Grey silent fragments

Of a grey silent world.

I listened in emptiness on the moor-ridge.
The curlew's tear turned its edge on the silence.

Slowly detail leafed from the darkness. Then the sun
Orange, red, red erupted

Silently, and splitting to its core tore and flung cloud,
Shook the gulf open, showed blue,

And the big planets hanging—.
I turned

Stumbling in the fever of a dream, down towards
The dark woods, from the kindling tops,

And came to the horses.
                              There, still they stood,
But now steaming and glistening under the flow of light,

Their draped stone manes, their tilted hind-hooves
Stirring under a thaw while all around them

The frost showed its fires. But still they made no sound.
Not one snorted or stamped,

Their hung heads patient as the horizons,
High over valleys, in the red levelling rays—

In din of the crowded streets, going among the years, the faces,
May I still meet my memory in so lonely a place

Between the streams and the red clouds, hearing curlews,
Hearing the horizons endure.

PART TWO

A Few More Words

The thing that strikes one more than anything else about the modern world is its kaleidoscopic variety, its contrasts, its contradictions—what Robert Graves calls in the first poem in this section of the anthology 'the fewness, muchness, rareness, greatness of this endless only precious world'. The poems in Part Two are arranged in a particular way to illustrate this and to show also the great variety of expression and style of modern poetry. I have not in every case explained the reasons for the arrangement (why a particular poem follows another), as I have worked on the assumption that often the poems themselves will lead you to investigate this.

Regardless of which poems in this selection you are actually required to study, I suggest you read as many of them—especially the modern ones in Part One as well as Part Two—as you can find time for. Flick through the book occasionally and read whichever poem catches your eye. Even use *Inscapes* as a kind of bedside book (however odd or 'square' that sounds). I suggest this not because you will like every poem you read (why on earth should you?), but because I feel sure you will find much in them to interest and perhaps excite you.

It is true that poetry cannot be said to have any real usefulness, in the practical sense of the word. You cannot 'do' anything with a poem. But, when you read these poems, you will find at least two or perhaps three things they all have in common. First, they are all concerned with an experience of some kind—whether a fairly 'unimportant' one such as e.e. cummings's observation of a grasshopper jumping from one place to another or Christopher Cheek's cutting his hand on a bacon-slicing machine, or a pretty crucial one such as David Holbrook's wondering if there is any possibility of contact between himself and the other members of his family.

Second, you will find that in each case the poet has, through writing the poem, become more aware of what these experiences really mean to him.

And third, if the poem 'works' for you, you will have been made more aware of some experience of life which you yourself have either had and not really thought about, or not had and are now capable of understanding more completely if and when you do have it. I am sure of one thing: the more aware we are of experiences we and others go through in life, the more complete we are as people. Perhaps this is the 'use' of reading poetry. It certainly is the point of reading poetry.

Finally, make a point of reading the poems written by people of your own age. (You will find these marked with asterisks in the index.) Examine their reactions to experiences; check theirs against your own; and, if you feel inclined, try to 'formalize' or organize your own experiences into verse. You will be amazed at how carefully you will be thinking about these experiences and about how words work. In all probability, you will also find it an exciting experience in itself, and you will come to understand what poetry is all about; why people have been writing it for as long as people have used words; and why we shall go on doing so for as long as human beings exist on this earth.

R.M.

Warning to children

ROBERT GRAVES

Children, if you dare to think
Of the greatness, rareness, muchness,
Fewness of this precious only
Endless world in which you say
You live, you think of things like this:
Blocks of slate enclosing dappled
Red and green, enclosing tawny
Yellow nets, enclosing white
And black acres of dominoes,
Where a neat brown paper parcel
Tempts you to untie the string.
In the parcel a small island,
On the island a large tree,
On the tree a husky fruit.
Strip the husk and pare the rind off:
In the kernel you will see
Blocks of slate enclosed by dappled
Red and green, enclosed by tawny
Yellow nets, enclosed by white
And black acres of dominoes,
Where the same brown paper parcel—
Children, leave the string alone!
For who dares undo the parcel
Finds himself at once inside it,
On the island, in the fruit,
Blocks of slate about his head,
Finds himself enclosed by dappled
Green and red, enclosed by yellow
Tawny nets, enclosed by black
And white acres of dominoes,
With the same brown paper parcel
Still untied upon his knee.
And, if he then should dare to think
Of the fewness, muchness, rareness,
Greatness of this endless only
Precious world in which he says
He lives--he then unties the string.

Constantly risking absurdity

LAWRENCE FERLINGHETTI

Constantly risking absurdity

                  and death

whenever he performs

              above the heads

                    of his audience

the poet like an acrobat

          climbs on rime

               to a high wire of his own making

and balancing on eyebeams

            above a sea of faces

paces his way

          to the other side of day

performing entrechats

           and sleight-of-foot tricks

and other high theatrics

          and all without mistaking

any thing

        for what it may not be

For he's the super realist

        who must perforce perceive

    taut truth

        before the taking of each stance or step

in his supposed advance

        toward that still higher perch

where Beauty stands and waits

        with gravity

        to start her death-defying leap

And he

    a little charleychaplin man

        who may or may not catch

her fair eternal form

      spreadeagled in the empty air

of existence.

Handwritten annotations:

tongue twister → difficulty of tightrope / poem

both aim to go forward

→ Homeric similee / poet & tightrope walker

→ Typography — reflects sense of poem (b.199→)

always / firmly → tackle something so difficult / bare soul to public

poetry can be mocked / ridiculed

antitheses → solid act, ridiculous + self dissatisfaction

writes / composes → spectacle → intelligence

intellectually to superior

creation like tightrope walker cautiously edging across

ice/frost ∴ slippery, difficult

Rhyme - pun - used by poet / poem

aspires, creates

exposed to critical gaze of public

metaphor → few creators & many critical readers/ many critical

measure carefully → rhythm, metre

end of poem — works hard throughout day

acrobatic tricks

hard-play on words

+ foot (pun) to Iambic Pentameter

stage like theatrical acts

paradox → superior to all others — reaches clearly, really

by force

emphasis / alliteration integrity / above

inching way to poem → universal, eternal, beauty

step forward in creation of poem

unsure whether the line is an advance / correct / beautiful

∴ risking absurdity

resting place

→ falling to earth

② seriousness

→ climax

→ circus terms throughout

(The poet)

→ small / comic / pathetic man

may / may not succeed in creating beautiful poem

→ trapeze artist

→ from nothing form / order is created

→ Having exposed himself, the poet still risks ridicule

→ Poet perceives beauty / can transfer it to poem only with skill & talent

In broken images

ROBERT GRAVES

He is quick, thinking in clear images;
I am slow, thinking in broken images.

He becomes dull, trusting to his clear images;
I become sharp, mistrusting my broken images.

Trusting his images, he assumes their relevance;
Mistrusting my images, I question their relevance.

Assuming their relevance, he assumes the fact;
Questioning their relevance, I question the fact.

When the fact fails him, he questions his senses;
When the fact fails me, I approve my senses.

He continues quick and dull in his clear images;
I continue slow and sharp in my broken images.

He in a new confusion of his understanding;
I in a new understanding of my confusion.

This image or another

CONRAD AIKEN

This image or another, this quick choosing,
raindrop choosing a path through grains of sand
the blood-drop choosing its way, that the dead world
may wake and think or sleep and dream

This gesture or another, this quick action
the bough broken by the wind and flung down
the hand striking or touching, that the dead world
may know itself and forget itself

This memory or another, this brief picture
sunbeam on the shrivelled and frosted leaf
a world of selves trying to remember the self
Before the idea of self is lost—

Walk with me world, upon my right hand walk,
speak to me Babel, that I may strive to assemble
of all these syllables a single word
before the purpose of speech is gone.

Blue umbrellas

D. J. ENRIGHT

'The thing that makes a blue umbrella with its tail—
How do you call it?' you ask. Poorly and pale
Comes my answer. For all I can call it is peacock.

Now that you go to school, you will learn how we call all sorts of things;
How we mar great works by our mean recital.
You will learn, for instance, that Head Monster is not the gentleman's
    accepted title;
The blue-tailed eccentrics will be merely peacocks; the dead bird will
    no longer doze
Off till tomorrow's lark, for the letter has killed him.
The dictionary is opening, the gay umbrellas close.

    Oh our mistaken teachers!—
It was not a proper respect for words that we need,
But a decent regard for things, those older creatures and more real.
Later you may even resort to writing verse
To prove the dishonesty of names and their black greed—
To confess your ignorance, to expiate your crime, seeking one spell to
    lift another curse.
Or you may, more commodiously, spy on your children, busy
    discoverers,
Without the dubious benefit of rhyme.

The secret

DENISE LEVERTOV

Two girls discover
the secret of life
in a sudden line of
poetry.

I who don't know the
secret wrote
the line. They
told me

(through a third person)
they had found it

118

but not what it was,
not even
what line it was. No doubt
by now, more than a week
later, they have forgotten
the secret,

the line, the name of
the poem. I love them
for finding what
I can't find,

and for loving me
for the line I wrote,
and for forgetting it
so that

a thousand times, till death
finds them, they may
discover it again, in other
lines,

in other
happenings. And for
wanting to know it,
for

assuming there is
such a secret, yes,
for that
most of all.

Poetry is death cast out

SYDNEY CLOUTS

Poetry is death cast out
though it gives one chance to retaliate.
Death takes it but the poem moves
a little further beyond death's gate,

and I know the proof of this. Once walking
amongst bushes and lizard stones I found
a little further than I had thought
to go, a stream with a singing sound.

It may be either the large public events of today or private everyday incidents that concern the poet. In the first two poems which follow, William Plomer reacts to the assassination of President John F. Kennedy in 1963; and William Carlos Williams to the first flight into space by Major Yuri Gagarin in 1961. The three subsequent poems could hardly be of less public importance.

Shot at sight

WILLIAM PLOMER

Dallas! The name slaps
Its cards on the table,
Flashes a brassy brash
Probable fable
Of cold men and wild men,
Hard, bright, unstable.

Hands full of aces!
Heads full of Bourbon!
Dollars! And shark-shaped
Cars flash like platinum,
Oil kings and ranch queens
Lolling to chat in them!

To see him, well-meaning,
Willing and able,
Glide past in dry sunshine,
Precarious with power—
Young, but no safer
Than Lincoln or Gandhi!

A rifle at any man
Aimed is at all of us
Pointed, protruding
Out of a commonplace
Building, the killer
And motive both hidden.

The President passed us
With hope in his smiling:
What hope in the finger
Hooked on the trigger?
Oh, the hope that is hatred
For the better and bigger.

120

Now something colossal
Is seen to rise towering
From a dead politician:
Not the torch-bearing woman,
Hollow, metallic,
Who holds the false promise
Of impossible freedom,
But the image or dream
Of attainable good
All men have a hint of.
Its agents, when murdered,
Have the honour to make
That asset (our greatest)
Safe yet for a season.

Heel & toe to the end

WILLIAM CARLOS WILLIAMS

Gagarin says, in ecstasy,
he could have
gone on forever

he floated
ate and sang
and when he emerged from that

one hundred eight minutes off
the surface of
the earth he was smiling

Then he returned
to take his place
among the rest of us

from all that division and
subtraction a measure
toe and heel

heel and toe he felt
as if he had
been dancing

This is just to say

WILLIAM CARLOS WILLIAMS

I have eaten
the plums
that were in
the icebox

and which
you were probably
saving
for breakfast

Forgive me
they were delicious
so sweet
and so cold

The one that got away

LESLIE PICKETT

Don't talk to me about the one
That got away. You should
'Ave seen wot 'appened.
There I was, sitting there wiv me
Rod in one 'and, and a sammidge
In the uvver, minding me own
Business and then it 'appened.
Me old reel started flying round and
Me old rod bent over and then
Ping!
The bloody lot 'ad gone.
All me line 'ad gone orf me
Reel and me rod was still shaking
From the vibrashun w'en me line went
And me rod flicked back.
I was flabbergasted! I just sat
There wiv 'alf a sammidge in me
'And, and me mouf wide open.

122

Proletarian portrait

WILLIAM CARLOS WILLIAMS

A big young bareheaded woman
in an apron

Her hair slicked back standing
on the street

One stockinged foot toeing
the sidewalk

Her shoe in her hand. Looking
intently into it

She pulls out the paper insole
to find the nail

That has been hurting her

How much need a poet have to say? Does William Carlos Williams's note
This is just to say, for example, qualify as poetry? Is the sharpness, the cleanness
of this expression of personal delight enough to justify it as a poem? Or the
ordinary everyday observation of Proletarian portrait? And what of these next
poems? A far cry from Gagarin's epic flight around the earth are these des-
criptions of a grasshopper jumping from a to b, a snail crawling through the
grass, and a praying mantis sitting on a leaf:

r-p-o-p-h-e-s-s-a-g-r

e. e. cummings

r-p-o-p-h-e-s-s-a-g-r

who

a)s w(e loo)k
upnowgath
                PPEGORHRASS
                            eringint(o-
aThe):l
        eA
          !p:
S   a
              (r
rIvInG   .gRrEaPsPhOs)
                            to
rea(be)rran(com)gi(e)ngly
,grasshopper;

That was really a technical exercise: it is a poet's attempt to convey a simple experience he has had — watching the grasshopper's leap — through an ingenious arrangement of words and letters. If you bear in mind the sort of awkward, jerky movements grasshoppers make, the changing visual shape they give, it is not too difficult to see how cummings reproduces the animal's jump in terms of typography. Notice, for instance, how the letters which make up the word 'grasshopper' become, each time they are used, a little closer to the correct letter-order until the grasshopper has finally settled down after its jump. And notice that marvellous moment of impact when the grasshopper lands and does a little bounce until the full-stop settles him on the ground.

Considering the snail

THOM GUNN

The snail pushes through a green
night, for the grass is heavy
with water and meets over
the bright path he makes, where rain
has darkened the earth's dark. He
moves in a wood of desire,

pale antlers barely stirring
as he hunts. I cannot tell
what power is at work, drenched there
with purpose, knowing nothing.
What is a snail's fury? All
I think is that if later

I parted the blades above
the tunnel and saw the thin
trail of broken white across
litter, I would never have
imagined the slow passion
to that deliberate progress.

Mantis

ROBERT DEDERICK

Green as an early leaf in Spring
He was, and no less green for being
Caught green-handed on an Autumn day
When puckered browns were everywhere.
My looming shadow held him there

In such a zone of worry as may
Make the least inclined to prayer
Suddenly inclined to pray.
It is improbable of course
That he could take the longer view
Beyond my local whelm of force
And pray in aid some primal Cause
Of whose effects we two were two;
Yet demonstrably there he was,
Clasping each green hand in each—
First in my shadow as if to beseech
And later, when my shadow withdrew,
As if in such thanksgiving mood
As those least given to gratitude
Are not entirely stranger to.

Perhaps it is poems like those two which make one say that poets see and reveal the 'essence' of things. But where does one expect to experience these insights? Only in the open fields or when in direct touch with nature? Why not at a Karroo siding or at the scene of an accident?

Karroo stop

SYDNEY CLOUTS

A whole
trainful of coal
like a soul
burnt black in a hole
or tunnel, passed us slowly.
We were halted in our carriage. The roll,
roll, roll, roll, roll, roll, roll,
dragged painfully, each truck like the goal
achieved, yet still this kept control
of each eye.

   A horse and a foal
beyond were meagre to it, coal-
black horse and foal,
and far-off clouds stroll white
in little mounds, and the coal
in mounds and piles that crawl
and crawl.

A sigh, a grunt from us all,
with one exception: I saw patrol
like a mole
underground, through walls
of skewer patience, cold and fire,
an old old
man's sharp smile, an old
man wrinkled small
with teeth like coal.

Auto wreck

Its quick soft silver bell beating, beating,
And down the dark one ruby flare
Pulsing out red light like an artery,
The ambulance at top speed floating down
Past beacons and illuminated clocks
Wings in a heavy curve, dips down,
And brakes speed, entering the crowd.
The doors leap open, emptying light;
Stretchers are laid out, the mangled lifted
And stowed into the little hospital.
Then the bell, breaking the hush, tolls once,
And the ambulance with its terrible cargo
Rocking, slightly rocking, moves away,
As the doors, an afterthought, are closed.

We are deranged, walking among the cops
Who sweep glass and are large and composed.
One is still making notes under the light.
One with a bucket douches ponds of blood
Into the street and gutter.
One hangs lanterns on the wrecks that cling,
Empty husks of locusts, to iron poles.

Our throats were tight as tourniquets,
Our feet were bound with splints, but now,
Like convalescents intimate and gauche,
We speak through sickly smiles and warn
With the stubborn saw of common sense,

126

The grim joke and the banal resolution.
The traffic moves around with care,
But we remain, touching a wound
That opens to our richest horror.

Already old, the question Who shall die?
Becomes unspoken Who is innocent?
For death in war is done by hands;
Suicide has cause and stillbirth, logic;
And cancer, simple as a flower, blooms.
But this invites the occult mind,
Cancels our physics with a sneer,
And spatters all we knew of denouement
Across the expedient and wicked stones.

Gertrude Stein once wrote a poem which said, 'A rose is a rose is a rose.' And she had a point. But, of course, people can and do look differently at the same thing. At snakes, for instance:

A narrow fellow in the grass

EMILY DICKINSON

A narrow fellow in the grass
Occasionally rides;
You may have met him,—did you not?
His notice sudden is.

The grass divides as with a comb,
A spotted shaft is seen;
And then it closes at your feet
And opens further on.

He likes a boggy acre,
A floor too cool for corn.
Yet when a boy, and barefoot,
I more than once, at noon,

Have passed, I thought, a whip-lash
Unbraiding in the sun,—
When, stooping to secure it,
It wrinkled, and was gone.

127

Several of nature's people
I know, and they know me;
I feel for them a transport
Of cordiality;

But never met this fellow,
Attended or alone,
Without a tighter breathing,
And zero at the bone.

Leviathan

DOUGLAS LIVINGSTONE

A puff-adder, khaki,
fatter than a stocking of pus
except for its short thin tail,
obese and quick
as certain light footed dancers
took a dozing lizard.

Scaly little monster
with delicate hands and feet
stupidly sluggish in the sun.
Panting, true,
but lizards breathe mostly
as if their lives depended.

Gone.
Enveloped by a slack
wormy yellow bowel.

O Jonah, to tumble to
those sickly deadly depths,
slick walled, implacably black.

In the snake park

WILLIAM PLOMER

A white-hot midday in the Snake Park.
Lethargy lay here and there in coils,
And here and there a neat obsidian head
Lay dreaming on a plaited yellow pillow of its own
Loops like a pretzel or a true-love knot.

A giant Python seemed a heap of tyres;
Two Nielsen's Vipers looked for a way out,
Sick of their cage and one another's curves;
And the long Ringsnake brought from Lembuland
Poured slowly through an opening like smoke.

Leaning intently forward a young girl
Discerned in stagnant water on a rock
A dark brown shoestring or discarded whiplash,
Then read the label to find out the name,
Then stared again: it moved. She screamed.

Old Piet Vander leant with us that day
On the low wall around the rocky space
Where amid broken quartz that cast no shade
Snakes twitched or slithered, or appeared to sleep,
Or lay invisible in the singing glare.

The sun throbbed like a fever as he spoke:
'Look carefully at this shrub with glossy leaves.
Leaves bright as brass. 'That leaf on top
Just there, do you see that it has eyes?
That's a Green Mamba, and it's watching *you*.

'A man I once knew did survive the bite,
Saved by a doctor running with a knife,
Serum and all. He was never the same again.
Vomiting blackness, agonizing, passing blood,
Part paralysed, near gone, he felt

'(He told me later) he would burst apart;
But the worst agony was in his mind—
Unbearable nightmare, worse than total grief
Or final loss of hope, impossibly magnified
To a blind passion of panic and extreme distress.'

Why should that little head have power
To inject all horror for no reason at all?'
'Ask me another—and beware of snakes.'
The sun was like a burning-glass. Face down
The girl who screamed had fallen in a faint.

Each of those reactions is different from the other — and each quite different from D. H. Lawrence's Snake *(p. 64).*

Read Hawk roosting *(p. 107), then these four poems about birds:*

A bird came down the walk

EMILY DICKINSON

A bird came down the walk:
He did not know I saw;
He bit an angle-worm in halves
And ate the fellow, raw.

And then he drank a dew
From a convenient grass,
And then hopped sidewise to the wall
To let a beetle pass.

He glanced with rapid eyes
That hurried all around—
They looked like frightened beads, I thought.
He stirred his velvet head

Like one in danger; cautious,
I offered him a crumb,
And he unrolled his feathers
And rowed him softer home

Than oars divide the ocean,
Too silver for a seam,
Or butterflies, off banks of noon,
Leap, plashless, as they swim.

Lake morning in autumn

DOUGLAS LIVINGSTONE

Before sunrise the stork was there
resting the pillow of his body
on stick legs growing from the water.

A flickering gust of pencil-slanted rain
swept over the chill autumn morning;
and he, too tired to arrange

his wind-buffeted plumage,
perched swaying a little,
neck flattened, ruminative,

130

beak on chest, contemplative eye
filmy with star vistas and hollow
black migratory league, strangely,

ponderously alone and some weeks
early. The dawn struck and everything,
sky, water, bird, reeds

was blood and gold. He sighed.
Stretching his wings he clubbed
the air; slowly, regally, so very tired,

aiming his beak he carefully climbed
inclining to his invisible tunnel of sky,
his feet trailing a long, long time.

Secretary bird

ALAN ROSS

Its name describes it, even to those penholder patches
Behind pale ears, the desiccated manner, head tilted
Back, offended, supercilious as it scratches
The scrub for snakes, faltering on stork-stilted
Legs feathered grey-black with tatty patches.

No other name could so well have drawn
Forth the image, as I saw it, near Philippolis, alone
Among thorn-bushes, in the red earth sharp stones
And waterwheels glinting, but in the whole Karoo
Only it moving, though abstracted, wondering what to do.

Since Kroonstad, 500 miles back, nothing so human
Had stirred in the desert, no man nor carrying woman,
So that stopping my car I had jumped it nearer
Through glasses, as on inadequate legs it came clearer,
Uncertainly swerving, as if blown by the dust.

And something about that haphazard swerve must
Have caught my memory, jolting me suddenly back
To a sailboat of a girl, quite incongruously unlike
It, but who moved so—indelibly so—
Through a part of my life, a long time ago.
I smiled at the absurdity, to find, as I let
In the clutch, my cheeks unaccountably wet.

Emerald dove

ANTHONY DELIUS

The Xhosa say
When the emerald dove
Sits sobbing in the bush
She is thinking of the terrible wars
And she cries
My father is dead
My mother is dead
My sisters are dead
My brothers are all dead
And my heart goes
Doem Doem
Doem doem doem doem
doem
doem.

These two 'feline' poems counterbalance D. H. Lawrence's Mountain lion
(p. 68):

The king

DOUGLAS LIVINGSTONE

Old Tawny's mane is moth-
eaten now, a balding monk's tonsure,
and his fluid thigh muscles flop
slack as an exhausted boxer's;

Creaks a little and is
just a fraction under fast (he's lame)
in those last short lethal rushes
at the slim white-eyed winging game;

Can catch them still of course,
the horny old claws combing crimson
from the velvet flanks in long scores,
here in the game-park's environs.

Each year, panting heavily,
manages with aged urbanity
to smile full-faced and yellowly
at a thousand box cameras.

132

Esther's tomcat

TED HUGHES

Daylong this tomcat lies stretched flat
As an old rough mat, no mouth and no eyes.
Continual wars and wives are what
Have tattered his ears and battered his head.

Like a bundle of old rope and iron
Sleeps till blue dusk. Then reappear
His eyes, green as ringstones: he yawns wide red,
Fangs fine as a lady's needle and bright.

A tomcat sprang at mounted knight,
Locked round his neck like a trap of hooks
While the knight rode fighting its clawing and bite.
After hundreds of years the stain's there

On the stone where he fell, dead of the tom:
That was at Barnborough. The tomcat still
Grallochs odd dogs on the quiet,
Will take the head clean off your simple pullet,

Is unkillable. From the dog's fury,
From gunshot fired point-blank he brings
His skin whole, and whole
From owlish moons of bekittenings

Among ashcans. He leaps and lightly
Walks upon sleep, his mind on the moon.
Nightly over the round world of men,
Over the roofs go his eyes and outcry.

People often say admiringly of animals that 'they are almost human': sometimes one wonders whether the compliment would not be more appropriate if reversed:

From Song of Myself

WALT WHITMAN

I think I could turn and live with animals, they are so placid and
    self-contain'd,
I stand and look at them long and long.

They do not sweat and whine about their condition,
They do not lie awake in the dark and weep for their sins,
They do not make me sick discussing their duty to God,
Not one is dissatisfied, not one is demented with the mania of owning
    things,
Not one kneels to another; nor to his kind that lived thousands of
    years ago,
Not one is respectable or unhappy over the whole earth.

[handwritten: → must live - not always rationalize]
[handwritten: → too proud of intellect ∴ can't know & experience original life force]

Lizard *[handwritten: → reptile, scaly, movable eyelids   reform society / - like a prehistoric animal / → Lawrence wants man "to be"]*

D. H. LAWRENCE

A lizard ran out on a rock and looked up, listening *[handwritten: → content just to live]*
no doubt to the sounding of the spheres. *[handwritten: Nature - me believe of music / → created by the planet]*
And what a dandy fellow! the right toss of a chin for you *[handwritten: difficult heard & unnatural man → elemental force beyond man]*
and swirl of a tail! *[handwritten: (a fop & positive) → small, self possessed first rate / → superiority for man to nature ...]*

If men were as much men as lizards are lizards *[handwritten: → man are only ½ man ½ lizard / ignore sexual drive]*
they'd be worth looking at. *[handwritten: → natural, content / man is too care-brave, not whole, healthy people]*

*Each of the next four poems is written by a South African and each is a different
reaction to being in a particular place:*

Transvaal afternoon *(Part 1 of* In the Lowveld)

C. J. DRIVER

The tall white house stands silently
In the heat of a Transvaal afternoon,
Between the mountain and the water,
Halfway between the sun and the trees.
Insects move slowly across the heat.
          There is danger of fire
In the pinetrees around my home:
You can see the farm-men look up,
Every now and again, watching for smoke;
The women keep their heads down.
All you hear is earth moving, cars
Across the river on the road
Through the plantations, and the drone
Of heat-flies. Up at my home
It would be cooler, for the air moves

Where the land lifts. But here,
Even your hands sweat. The sun
Slaps down across the lowveld.
                    Nothing
Has much meaning here, where the sun
Strikes. The red dust is still, tickbirds
Sit in a tree above the water, men
And women working do not talk,
Even curse the heat. The sun gropes
At your body and at the lowveld.
                    But later,
When I go home, the lowveld will close
Around me, and the wind will move
Suddenly through the house.

Blue stuff

DOUGLAS LIVINGSTONE

Wall-to-wall city on a rainy night: eleven
stories up and the wonder-hour-hand when
is 4 a.m. with only a very quiet Kenton
accompanying the one sky-lamp in

the corner. Yes, she's gone, warm to bed.
The floor feels strangely concrete-solid
despite the undermining gusts walled outside.
Wet beetles lie parked under street lamps, dead.

The wakeful rain musics back no April
in Paris, nor stale old Stars fell
on Alabama. Somewhere, space unfurls
its furnaced seasons. Somewhere, over the sill,

crooked as the iced-sucker wrapper flies,
the holiday surf, swelled into its own says:
The sshun'sh gone. The night-tide ebbs and soughs
loud and lording it unchallenged upon the shores

of South Beach, North Beach, Country Club.
Even the sherry-drinkers have long stubbed
the last drag. The street's hands are cupped;
the stars, maybe forever, are all washed up.

The wild doves at Louis Trichardt

Morning is busy with long files
Of ants and men, all bearing loads.
The sun's gong beats, and sweat runs down.
A mason-hornet shapes his hanging house.
In a wide flood of flowers
Two crested cranes are bowing to their food.
From the north today there is ominous news.

Midday, the mad cicada-time.
Sizzling from every open valve
Of the overheated earth
The stridulators din it in—
Intensive and continuing praise
Of the white-hot zenith, shrilling on
Toward a note too high to bear.

Oven of afternoon, silence of heat.
In shadow, or in shaded rooms,
This face is hidden in folded arms,
That face is now a sightless mask,
Tree-shadow just includes those legs.
The people have all lain down, and sleep
In attitudes of the sick, the shot, the dead.

And now in the grove the wild doves begin,
Whose neat silk heads are never still,
Bubbling their coolest colloquies.
The formulae they liquidly pronounce
In secret tents of leaves imply
(Clearer than man-made music could)
Men being absent, Africa is good.

Stranger to Europe

GUY BUTLER

Stranger to Europe, waiting release,
My heart a torn-up, drying root
I breathed the rain of an Irish peace

136

That afternoon when a bird or a tree,
Long known as an exiled name, could cease
As such, take wing and trembling shoot
Green light and shade through the heart of me.

Near a knotty hedge we had stopped.
'This is an aspen.' 'Tell me more.'
Customary veils and masks had dropped.
Each looked at the hidden other in each.
Sure, we who could never kiss had leapt
To living conclusions long before
Golden chestnut or copper beech.

So, as the wind drove sapless leaves
Into the bonfire of the sun,
As thunderclouds made giant graves
Of the black, bare hills of Kerry,
In a swirl of shadow, words, one by one
Fell on the stubble and the sheaves;
'Wild dogrose this; this, hawthorn berry.'

But there was something more you meant,
As if the trees and clouds had grown
Into a timeless flame that burnt
All worlds of words and left them dust
Through stubble and sedge by the late wind blown:
A love not born and not to be learnt,
But given and taken, an ultimate trust.

Now, between my restless eyes
And the scribbled wisdom of the ages
Black hills meet moving skies
And through rough hedges a late wind blows;
And in my palm through all the rages
Of lust and love now, always, lie
Brown hawthorn berry, red dogrose.

Wherever they may be, few in the twentieth century have been able to avoid being either indirectly or personally involved in war. Young men went off to the First World War — 'the war to end all war' — with a boldness of spirit and a sense of the nobility and honour of what they were doing. Rupert Brooke (who died at the age of 28 while serving in the Aegean in 1915) was the main voice of this mood:

Peace

RUPERT BROOKE

Now, God be thanked Who has matched us with His hour,
   And caught our youth, and wakened us from sleeping,
With hand made sure, clear eye, and sharpened power,
   To turn, as swimmers into cleanness leaping,
Glad from a world grown old and cold and weary,
   Leave the sick hearts that honour could not move,
And half-men, and their dirty songs and dreary,
   And all the little emptiness of love!

Oh! we, who have known shame, we have found release there,
   Where there's no ill, no grief, but sleep has mending.
     Naught broken save this body, lost but breath;
Nothing to shake the laughing heart's long peace there
   But only agony, and that has ending;
     And the worst friend and enemy is but Death.

But another, more powerful, voice was that of Wilfred Owen, who, aged 25, was killed in action exactly one week before the war ended in November 1918. (See also other poems by Owen, pp. 75-9.)

The sentry

WILFRED OWEN

We'd found an old Boche dug-out, and he knew,
And gave us hell, for shell on frantic shell
Hammered on top, but never quite burst through.
Rain, guttering down in waterfalls of slime
Kept slush waist-high and rising hour by hour,
And choked the steps too thick with clay to climb.
What murk of air remained stank old, and sour
With fumes of whizz-bangs, and the smell of men
Who'd lived there years, and left their curse in the den,
If not their corpses. . . .

138

There we herded from the blast

Of whizz-bangs, but one found our door at last,—
Buffeting eyes and breath, snuffing the candles.
And thud! flump! thud! down the steep steps came thumping
And sploshing in the flood, deluging muck—
The sentry's body; then, his rifle, handles
Of old Boche bombs, and mud in ruck on ruck.
We dredged him up, for killed, until he whined
'O sir, my eyes—I'm blind—I'm blind, I'm blind!'
Coaxing, I held a flame against his lids
And said if he could see the least blurred light
He was not blind; in time he'd get all right.
'I can't,' he sobbed. Eyeballs, huge-bulged like squids'
Watch my dreams still; but I forgot him there
In posting Next for duty, and sending a scout
To beg a stretcher somewhere, and flound'ring about
To other posts under the shrieking air.

Those other wretches, how they bled and spewed,
And one who would have drowned himself for good,—
I try not to remember these things now.
Let dread hark back for one word only: how
Half listening to that sentry's moans and jumps,
And the wild chattering of his broken teeth,
Renewed most horribly whenever crumps
Pummelled the roof and slogged the air beneath—
Through the dense din, I say, we heard him shout
'I see your lights!' But ours had long died out.

Here is what happens when rifles and flowers are suddenly put into the same context:

Naming of parts

HENRY REED

Today we have naming of parts. Yesterday,
We had daily cleaning. And tomorrow morning,
We shall have what to do after firing. But today,
Today we have naming of parts. Japonica
Glistens like coral in all of the neighbouring gardens,
　　And today we have naming of parts.

139

This is the lower sling swivel. And this
Is the upper sling swivel, whose use you will see,
When you are given your slings. And this is the piling swivel,
Which in your case you have not got. The branches
Hold in the gardens their silent, eloquent gestures,
    Which in our case we have not got.

This is the safety-catch, which is always released
With an easy flick of the thumb. And please do not let me
See anyone using his finger. You can do it quite easy
If you have any strength in your thumb. The blossoms
Are fragile and motionless, never letting anyone see
    Any of them using their finger.

And this you can see is the bolt. The purpose of this
Is to open the breech, as you see. We can slide it
Rapidly backwards and forwards: we call this
Easing the spring. And rapidly backwards and forwards
The early bees are assaulting and fumbling the flowers:
    They call it easing the Spring.

They call it easing the Spring: it is perfectly easy
If you have any strength in your thumb: like the bolt,
And the breech, and the cocking-piece, and the point of balance,
Which in our case we have not got; and the almond-blossom
Silent in all of the gardens and the bees going backwards and forwards,
    For today we have naming of parts.

But is war all grim, all deadening, all dispiriting? A young Canadian sent home these lines written on the back of an envelope shortly before he was killed in action:

High flight

JOHN GILLESPIE MAGEE

Oh, I have slipped the surly bonds of earth,
And danced the skies on laughter-silvered wings;
Sunward I've climbed and joined the tumbling mirth
Of sun-split clouds—and done a hundred things
You have not dreamt of—wheeled and soared and swung
High in the sunlit silence. Hov'ring there,
I've chased the shouting wind along and flung
My eager craft through footless halls of air.

Up, up the long delirious burning blue
I've topped the wind-swept heights with easy grace,
Where never lark, or even eagle, flew;
And, while with silent, lifting mind I've trod
The high untrespassed sanctity of space,
Put out my hand, and touched the face of God.

(It is interesting to compare that poem with Yeats's An Irish airman foresees his death, *p. 57.)*
On 6 August 1945 the first Atomic Bomb was dropped on Hiroshima. 60,000 people were killed and 100,000 injured:

No more Hiroshimas

JAMES KIRKUP

At the station exit, my bundle in hand,
Early the winter afternoon's wet snow
Falls thinly round me, out of a crudded sun.
I had forgotten to remember where I was.
Looking about, I see it might be anywhere—
A station, a town like any other in Japan,
Ramshackle, muddy, noisy, drab; a cheerfully
Shallow permanence: peeling concrete, litter, 'Atomic
Lotion, for hair fall-out', a flimsy department-store;
Racks and towers of neon, flashy over tiled and tilted waves
Of little roofs, shacks cascading lemons and persimmons,
Oranges and dark-red apples, shanties awash with rainbows
Of squid and octopus, shellfish, slabs of tuna, oysters, ice,
Ablaze with fans of soiled nude-picture books
Thumbed abstractedly by schoolboys, with second-hand looks.

The river remains unchanged, sad, refusing rehabilitation.
In this long, wide, empty official boulevard
The new trees are still small, the office blocks
Basely functional, the bridge a slick abstraction.
But the river remains unchanged, sad, refusing rehabilitation.

In the city centre, far from the station's lively squalor,
A kind of life goes on, in cinemas and hi-fi coffee bars,
In the shuffling racket of pin-table palaces and parlours,
The souvenir-shops piled with junk, kimonoed kewpie-dolls,
Models of the bombed Industry Promotion Hall, memorial ruin
Tricked out with glitter-frost and artificial pearls.

Set in an awful emptiness, the modern tourist hotel is trimmed
With jaded Christmas frippery, flatulent balloons; in the hall,
A giant dingy iced cake in the shape of a Cinderella coach.
The contemporary stairs are treacherous, the corridors
Deserted, my room an overheated morgue, the bar in darkness.
Punctually, the electric chimes ring out across the tidy waste
Their doleful public hymn—the tune unrecognizable, evangelist.

Here atomic peace is geared to meet the tourist trade.
Let it remain like this, for all the world to see,
Without nobility or loveliness, and dogged with shame
That is beyond all hope of indignation. Anger, too, is dead.
And why should memorials of what was far
From pleasant have the grace that helps us to forget?

In the dying afternoon, I wander dying round the Park of Peace.
It is right, this squat, dead place, with its left-over air
Of an abandoned International Trade and Tourist Fair.
The stunted trees are wrapped in straw against the cold.
The gardeners are old, old women in blue bloomers, white aprons,
Survivors weeding the dead brown lawns around the Children's
   Monument.

A hideous pile, the Atomic Bomb Explosion Centre, freezing cold,
'Includes the Peace Tower, a museum containing
Atomic-melted slates and bricks, photos showing
What the Atomic Desert looked like, and other
Relics of the catastrophe.'

The other relics:
The ones that made me weep;
The bits of burnt clothing,
The stopped watches, the torn shirts.
The twisted buttons,
The stained and tattered vests and drawers,
The ripped kimonos and charred boots,
The white blouse polka-dotted with atomic rain, indelible,
The cotton summer pants the blasted boys crawled home in, to bleed
And slowly die.

Remember only these.
They are the memorials we need.

The writer of the next poem prefaces it with these words by the great Russian novelist Dostoievsky: 'And if the sufferings of children go to swell the sum of suffering which was necessary to pay for truth, then I protest that the truth is not worth such a price.' In the context of warfare, is such a statement justifiable?

On the mountain

M. K. JOSEPH

The bones of the children cried out upon the mountain
Thin bones, bird bones, crying like birds
Up the glacier birdfooted tracks
Hen's feet crows' feet, old snow old world.

The blood of the children cried out upon pavements
The burnt flesh of children screamed in the cities.
All over the earth machines stopped
Animals were dumb men stood listening
And this terrible crying accused
   The men in gold braid who make wars
   The men in silk hats who make peace
   The men in leather jackets who make revolutions
   The men in frock coats who break revolutions.

Then from His throne spoke the Lord Jehovah
Saying: bring Me millstones
A mountain of hollow stones for the necks
Of those who offended these My children.
And He was angry, saying: let there be ocean
Unplumbed depths, bewildering fishes
For each transgressor one halter and one stone.
The angry waves roared Aaaahhhhh.

Still the bones of the children cried out
The blood cried from the cobblestones
The paper bones glittering on ice
The honey blood swarming with blue flies.
By the ocean-sea walked the Lord Jehovah
Thinking milleniums; about His feet
Cherubim played ducks and drakes
With the hollow stones. The sea said Hussshhhh.

He heard the feet of a million walking
Unhurried, firm, from valley and plain
Before them ran trembling those to be judged
   Flapping and fumbling
   Mouthing and mumbling
   Stooping and stumbling

Over the icy stones
   The men with gold eyes
   The men with silk hands
   The men with leather hearts
   The men with no faces
To be judged: to be brought to judgement
Before the children's bones, on the holy mountain.

Where, ultimately, is modern war leading? And can modern man reconcile his warfare and his God? (Compare the first of the next three poems with T. S. Eliot's Triumphal march, *p. 74.)*

A prayer in the Pentagon

NINE
planets, Sir, endlessly circle, Sir,
one yellow star among Sir's galaxies:
Pluto Neptune Venus Jupiter
Saturn Uranus Mercury Mars and this—
this watered and this aired this favored one
where all that crawl and swim and fly and run
that drove and swarm and herd and flock are in
with tooth and leg and lung and claw and fin
created clothed and colored are by Sir

EIGHT
colors (counting white) Sir's rainbow makes
when whiteness on Sir's broken waters breaks
arched over tidal blue and branching grey
and grazing green and foaling brown down and away
with gorsing yellow glow and honeyed hay
and petalled blush and mottled winging whirr;
the limpid eyes each of Sir's colors wakes
dark-irised are and cleared and curved by Sir

144

SEVEN

tossing seas Sir's pent-up lands divide
where silver shoals in aching green-ness glide
turn suddenly and dart and flatly lie
break surface plunge and from each other hide
and stare as though by staring they aver
what sweet surprise had widened each wide eye
that once looked early on creating Sir

SIX

senses there were then in us who were
salt-tasting all along salt-scented shore
who felt crust cool and looked on shrinking sea
and heard gull-cry on draining estuary
and found back of these five a something more:
a sense of self and back of self—Sir

FIVE

fingers (counting a thumb) were what
we mostly were aware of as we fought
Sir's elements and cleared Sir's forests and sought
creation-wise new metalled ways to go
by spinning wheel and wing off runway. So?—

FOUR

quarters of our world began to grow
too few and of Sir's yellow star we thought
equations scribbled bubbled in retort
distilled its hot explosive secrets. So?—

THREE

questions pose themselves now as we wait:
did Sir not know how to end what Sir began?
Or could we choose? Or did Sir always plan

TWO

hands of ours to bring us soon or late
bent to destroy what hands of Sir's had wrought

ONE

day when we and all our world are brought to

NOUGHT?

Your attention please

PETER PORTER

The Polar DEW has just warned that
A nuclear rocket strike of
At least one thousand megatons
Has been launched by the enemy
Directly at our major cities.
This announcement will take
Two and a quarter minutes to make.
You therefore have a further
Eight and a quarter minutes
To comply with the shelter
Requirements published in the Civil
Defence Code—section Atomic Attack.
A specially shortened Mass
Will be broadcast at the end
Of this announcement—
Protestant and Jewish services
Will begin simultaneously—
Select your wavelength immediately
According to instructions
In the Defence Code. Do not
Take well-loved pets (including birds)
Into your shelter—they will consume
Fresh air. Leave the old and bed-
ridden, you can do nothing for them.
Remember to press the sealing
Switch when everyone is in
The shelter. Set the radiation
Aerial, turn on the geiger barometer.
Turn off your Television now.
Turn off your radio immediately
The Services end. At the same time
Secure explosion plugs in the ears
Of each member of your family. Take
Down your plasma flasks. Give your children
The pills marked one and two
In the C.D. green container, then put
Them to bed. Do not break
The inside airlock seals until

The radiation All Clear shows
(Watch for the Cuckoo in your
Perspex panel), or your District
Touring Doctor rings your bell.
If before this, your air becomes
Exhausted or if any member of your family
Is critically injured, administer
The capsules marked 'Valley Forge'
(Red pocket in No. 1 Survival Kit)
For painless death. (Catholics
Will have been instructed by their priests
What to do in this eventuality.)
This announcement is ending. Our President
Has already given orders for
Massive retaliation—it will be
Decisive. Some of us may die.
Remember, statistically
It is not likely to be you.
All flags are flying fully dressed
On Government buildings—the sun is shining.
Death is the least we have to fear.
We are all in the hands of God,
Whatever happens happens by His Will.
Now go quickly to your shelters.

The earth's atomic death

E. S. BLUMENTHAL

The swishing sound of the sea
On the dark night of Death.
The moon is pale.
The brazen breakers and the breeze
Sing prophetic songs of peace.
There is silence.
Then the sea,
The sea shouts with drowning voice,
Seagulls shriek, stones roll,
The earth trembles,
The waters roar.
The sky turns white,

Then black again.
Nox stands frozen
A monument.

A lone spirit walks
on the stony beach.
A lone voice sings.
'Tis Melpomene,
Singing in praise of Man.

(Note: Melpomene is the Muse of Tragedy.)

*However, until that happens, life goes on, as does the everyday business of
doing a job of work and earning a living. To what extent does it matter what
sort of social status we have? whether we are rich or poor?*

Psalm of those who go forth before daylight

CARL SANDBURG

The policeman buys shoes slow and careful; the teamster buys gloves
slow and careful; they take care of their feet and hands; they live
on their feet and hands.

The milkman never argues; he works alone and no one speaks to
him; the city is asleep when he is on the job; he puts a bottle on six
hundred porches and calls it a day's work; he climbs two hundred
wooden stairways; two horses are company for him; he never argues.

The rolling-mill men and the sheet-steel men are brothers of cinders;
they empty cinders out of their shoes after the day's work; they ask
their wives to fix burnt holes in the knees of their trousers; their
necks and ears are covered with a smut; they scour their necks and
ears; they are brothers of cinders.

After the opera

D. H. LAWRENCE

Down the stone stairs
Girls with their large eyes wide with tragedy
Lift looks of shocked and momentous emotion up at me.
And I smile.

.Ladies
Stepping like birds with their bright and pointed feet
Peer anxiously forth, as if for a boat to carry them out of the wreckage;
And among the wreck of the theatre crowd
I stand and smile.
They take tragedy so becomingly;
Which pleases me.

But when I meet the weary eyes
The reddened, aching eyes of the bar-man with thin arms,
I am glad to go back to where I came from.

Poverty

D. H. LAWRENCE

The only people I ever heard talk about my Lady Poverty
were rich people, or people who imagined themselves rich.
Saint Francis himself was a rich and spoiled young man.

Being born among the working people
I know that poverty is a hard old hag,
and a monster, when you're pinched for actual necessities.
And whoever says she isn't, is a liar.

I don't want to be poor, it means I am pinched.
But neither do I want to be rich.
When I look at this pine-tree near the sea,
that grows out of rock, and plumes forth, plumes forth,
. I see it has a natural abundance.

With its roots it has a grand grip on its daily bread,
and its plumes look like green cups held up to the sun and air
and full of wine.

I want to be like that, to have a natural abundance
and plume forth, and be splendid.

Anthony Delius knows the Cape well, and understands the Cape fishermen; just as Herman Bosman knew the Western Transvaal and understood the Marico farmer:

The gamblers

ANTHONY DELIUS

The Coloured long-shore fishermen unfurl
their nets beside the chilly and unrested sea,
and in their heads the little dawn-winds whirl
some scraps of gambling, drink and lechery.

Barefoot on withered kelp and broken shell,
they toss big baskets on the brittle turf,
then with a gambler's bitter patience still
slap down their wagering boat upon the surf.

Day flips a golden coin—but they mock it.
With calloused, careless hands they reach
deep down into the sea's capacious pocket
and pile their silver chips upon the beach.

Seed

H. C. BOSMAN

The farmer ploughs into the ground
More than the wheat-seed strewn on the ground
The farmer ploughs into the ground
The plough and the oxen and his body
He ploughs into the ground the farmstead and the cattle
And the pigs and the poultry and the kitchen utensils
And the afternoon sunlight shining into the window panes of the
   voorhuis
And the light entangled in the eyes of his children
He ploughs into the ground his wife's brown body
And the windmill above the borehole
And the borehole and the wind driving the windmill.
The farmer ploughs the blue clouds into the ground;
And as a tribute to the holocaust of the ploughshare—
To the sowing that was the parting of the Juggernaut—
The earth renders the farmer in due season
Corn.

Autumn on the land

R. S. THOMAS

A man, a field, silence—what is there to say?
He lives, he moves, and the October day
Burns slowly down.
         History is made
Elsewhere; the hours forfeit to time's blade
Don't matter here. The leaves large and small,
Shed by the branches, unlamented fall
About his shoulders. You may look in vain
Through the eyes' window; on his meagre hearth
The thin, shy soul has not begun its reign
Over the darkness. Beauty, love and mirth
And joy are strangers there.
         You must revise
Your bland philosophy of nature, earth
Has of itself no power to make men wise.

*How does Thomas's picture compare with Bosman's? or with the Words-
worthian figure of 'the man of the soil'?*

And what of other people and their various reactions to work and routine?

Last lesson of the afternoon

D. H. LAWRENCE

When will the bell ring, and end this weariness?
How long have they tugged the leash, and strained apart,
My pack of unruly hounds! I cannot start
Them again on a quarry of knowledge they hate to hunt,
I can haul them and urge them no more.

No longer now can I endure the brunt
Of the books that lie out on the desks; a full threescore
Of several insults of blotted pages, and scrawl
Of slovenly work they have offered me.
I am sick, and what on earth is the good of it all?
What good to them or me, I cannot see!

151

So, shall I take
My last dear fuel of life to heap on my soul
And kindle my will to a flame that shall consume
Their dross of indifference; and take the toll
Of their insults in punishment?—I will not!—

I will not waste my soul and my strength for this.
What do I care for all that they do amiss!
What is the point of this teaching of mine, and of this
Learning of theirs? It all goes down the same abyss.

What does it matter to me, if they can write
A description of a dog, or if they can't?
What is the point? To us both, it is all my aunt!
And yet I'm supposed to care, with all my might.

I do not, and will not; they won't and they don't; and that's all!
I shall keep my strength for myself; they can keep theirs as well.
Why should we beat our heads against the wall
Of each other? I shall sit and wait for the bell.

The best of school

D. H. LAWRENCE

The blinds are drawn because of the sun,
And the boys and the room in a colourless gloom
Of underwater float: bright ripples run
Across the walls as the blinds are blown
To let the sunlight in; and I,
As I sit on the shores of the class, alone,
Watch the boys in their summer blouses
As they write, their round heads busily bowed:
And one after another rouses
His face to look at me,
To ponder very quietly,
As seeing, he does not see.

And then he turns again, with a little, glad
Thrill of his work he turns again from me,
Having found what he wanted, having got what was to be had.
And very sweet it is, while the sunlight waves

In the ripening morning, to sit alone with the class
And feel the stream of awakening ripple and pass
From me to the boys, whose brightening souls it laves
For this little hour.

This morning, sweet it is
To feel the lads' looks light on me,
Then back in a swift, bright flutter to work;
Each one darting away with his
Discovery, like birds that steal and flee.

Touch after touch I feel on me
As their eyes glance at me for the grain
Of rigour they taste delightedly.

As tendrils reach out yearningly,
Slowly rotate till they touch the tree
That they cleave unto, and up which they climb
Up to their lives—so they to me.

I feel them cling and cleave to me
As vines going eagerly up; they twine
My life with other leaves, my time
Is hidden in theirs, their thrills are mine.

Warning

JENNY JOSEPH

When I am an old woman I shall wear purple
With a red hat which doesn't go, and doesn't suit me,
And I shall spend my pension on brandy and summer gloves
And satin sandals, and say we've no money for butter.
I shall sit down on the pavement when I'm tired
And gobble up samples in shops and press alarm bells
And run my stick along the public railings
And make up for the sobriety of my youth.
I shall go out in my slippers in the rain
And pick the flowers in other people's gardens
And learn to spit.

You can wear terrible shirts and grow more fat
And eat three pounds of sausages at a go
Or only bread and pickle for a week
And hoard pens and pencils and beermats and things in boxes.

153

But now we must have clothes that keep us dry
And pay our rent and not swear in the street
And set a good example for the children.
We will have friends to dinner and read the papers.

But maybe I ought to practise a little now?
So people who know me are not too shocked and surprised
When suddenly I am old and start to wear purple.

Toads

PHILIP LARKIN

Why should I let the toad *work*
    Squat on my life?
Can't I use my wit as a pitchfork
    And drive the brute off?

Six days of the week it soils
    With its sickening poison—
Just for paying a few bills!
    That's out of proportion.

Lots of folk live on their wits:
    Lecturers, lispers,
Losels, loblolly-men, louts—
    They don't end as paupers.

Lots of folk live up lanes
    With fires in a bucket;
Eat windfalls and tinned sardines—
    They seem to like it.

Their nippers have got bare feet,
    Their unspeakable wives
Are skinny as whippets—and yet
    No one actually *starves*.

Ah, were I courageous enough
    To shout *Stuff your pension!*
But I know, all too well, that's the stuff
    That dreams are made on:

For something sufficiently toad-like
  Squats in me too;
Its hunkers are heavy as hard luck,
  And cold as snow,

And will never allow me to blarney
  My way to getting
The fame and the girl and the money
  All at one sitting.

I don't say, one bodies the other
  One's spiritual truth;
But I do say it's hard to lose either
  When you have both.

Sunstrike

DOUGLAS LIVINGSTONE

A solitary prospector
staggered, locked in a vision
of slate hills that capered
on the molten horizon.

Waterless, he came to where
a river had run, now a band
flowing only in ripples
of white unquenchable sand.

Cursing, he dug sporadically
here, here, as deep as his arm,
and sat quite still, eyes thirstily
incredulous on his palm.

A handful of alluvial
diamonds leered back, and more: mixed
in the scar, glinted globules
of rubies, emeralds, onyx.

And then he was swimming in fire
and drinking, splashing hot halos
of glittering drops at the choir
of assembled carrion crows.

155

A person's hold on his work — and even on life — is perhaps precarious. He may be overtaken by injury, however slight or devastating; or by death, however quiet or unexpected. The following poems revolve around these issues in varying moods and at different levels:

Accident

CHRISTOPHER CHEEK

Ahh! at last, nearly five-thirty.
Now just the long leisurely cleaning of the bacon machine
All keen, I'll grease the wheel.
One bit of odd fat and round and round like french polishing
Gently to the blade, no blood, no pain, how neat
But off again as quick as lightning.
Go to the office
Interrupt manager—sacrilege.
'O.K. son I'm a St John's man you know'—pompous to the last.

Masses of blood now,
Still no pain—cheated.
'Sorry about the blood on your floor'—crawl to the last.
Now the reward—the shop girls
'Oh my poor dear—does it hurt?'
Wince
'Well you know'
Wince again
'Only a little'
Oh boy! great—
Perhaps a scar to talk about
Shivering with excitement.
'Come on son I'll give you a lift to the hospital.'

'Butch' Weldy

EDGAR LEE MASTERS

After I got religion and steadied down
They gave me a job in the canning works,
And every morning I had to fill
The tank in the yard with gasoline,
That fed the blow-fires in the sheds
To heat the soldering irons.
And I mounted a rickety ladder to do it,

156

Carrying buckets full of the stuff.
One morning, as I stood there pouring,
The air grew still and seemed to heave,
And I shot up as the tank exploded,
And down I came with both legs broken,
And my eyes burned crisp as a couple of eggs
For someone left a blow-fire going,
And something sucked the flame in the tank.
The Circuit Judge said whoever did it
Was a fellow-servant of mine, and so
Old Rhodes' son didn't have to pay me.
And I sat on the witness stand as blind
As Jack the Fiddler, saying over and over,
'I didn't know him at all.'

'Out, out—'

ROBERT FROST

The buzz saw snarled and rattled in the yard
And made dust and dropped stove-length sticks of wood,
Sweet-scented stuff when the breeze drew across it.
And from there those that lifted eyes could count
Five mountain ranges one behind the other
Under the sunset far into Vermont.
And the saw snarled and rattled, snarled and rattled,
As it ran light, or had to bear a load.
And nothing happened: day was all but done.
Call it a day, I wish they might have said
To please the boy by giving him the half hour
That a boy counts so much when saved from work.
His sister stood beside them in her apron
To tell them 'Supper'. At the word, the saw,
As if to prove saws knew what supper meant,
Leaped out at the boy's hand, or seemed to leap—
He must have given the hand. However it was,
Neither refused the meeting. But the hand!
The boy's first outcry was a rueful laugh,
As he swung toward them holding up the hand
Half in appeal, but half as if to keep
The life from spilling. Then the boy saw all—

Since he was old enough to know, big boy
Doing a man's work, though a child at heart—
He saw all spoiled. 'Don't let him cut my hand off—
The doctor, when he comes. Don't let him, sister!'
So. But the hand was gone already.
The doctor put him in the dark of ether.
He lay and puffed his lips out with his breath.
And then—the watcher at his pulse took fright.
No one believed. They listened at his heart.
Little—less—nothing!—and that ended it.
No more to build on there. And they, since they
Were not the one dead, turned to their affairs.

The bustle in a house

EMILY DICKINSON

The bustle in a house
The morning after death
Is solemnest of industries
Enacted upon earth,—

The sweeping up the heart,
And putting love away
We shall not want to use again
Until eternity.

The death of the hired man

ROBERT FROST

Mary sat musing on the lamp-flame at the table
Waiting for Warren. When she heard his step,
She ran on tiptoe down the darkened passage
To meet him in the doorway with the news
And put him on his guard. 'Silas is back.'
She pushed him outward with her through the door
And shut it after her. 'Be kind,' she said.
She took the market things from Warren's arms
And set them on the porch, then drew him down
To sit beside her on the wooden steps.

'When was I ever anything but kind to him?
But I'll not have the fellow back,' he said.

'I told him so last haying, didn't I?
If he left then, I said, that ended it.
What good is he? Who else will harbour him
At his age for the little he can do?
What help he is there's no depending on.
Off he goes always when I need him most.
He thinks he ought to earn a little pay,
Enough at least to buy tobacco with,
So he won't have to beg and be beholden.
"All right," I say, "I can't afford to pay
Any fixed wages, though I wish I could."
"Someone else can." "Then someone else will have to."
I shouldn't mind him bettering himself
If that was what it was. You can be certain,
When he begins like that, there's someone at him
Trying to coax him off with pocket-money,—
In haying time, when any help is scarce.
In winter he comes back to us. I'm done.'

'Sh! not so loud: he'll hear you,' Mary said.

'I want him to: he'll have to soon or late.'

'He's worn out. He's asleep beside the stove.
When I came up from Rowe's I found him here,
Huddled against the barn-door fast asleep,
A miserable sight, and frightening, too—
You needn't smile—I didn't recognize him—
I wasn't looking for him—and he's changed.
Wait till you see.'
                    'Where did you say he'd been?'

'He didn't say. I dragged him to the house,
And gave him tea and tried to make him smoke.
I tried to make him talk about his travels.
Nothing would do: he just kept nodding off.'

'What did he say? Did he say anything?'

'But little.'

            'Anything? Mary, confess
He said he'd come to ditch the meadow for me.'

'Warren!'

       'But did he? I just want to know.'

'Of course he did. What would you have him say?
Surely you wouldn't grudge the poor old man
Some humble way to save his self-respect.
He added, if you really care to know,
He meant to clear the upper pasture, too.
That sounds like something you have heard before?
Warren, I wish you could have heard the way
He jumbled everything. I stopped to look
Two or three times—he made me feel so queer—
To see if he was talking in his sleep.
He ran on Harold Wilson—you remember—
The boy you had in haying four years since.
He's finished school, and teaching in his college.
Silas declares you'll have to get him back.
He says they two will make a team for work:
Between them they will lay this farm as smooth!
The way he mixed that in with other things.
He thinks young Wilson a likely lad, though daft
On education—you know how they fought
All through July under the blazing sun,
Silas up on the cart to build the load,
Harold along beside to pitch it on.'

'Yes, I took care to keep well out of earshot.'

'Well, those days trouble Silas like a dream.
You wouldn't think they would. How some things linger!
Harold's young college boy's assurance piqued him.
After so many years he still keeps finding
Good arguments he sees he might have used.
I sympathize. I know just how it feels
To think of the right thing to say too late.
Harold's associated in his mind with Latin.
He asked me what I thought of Harold's saying
He studied Latin like the violin
Because he liked it—that an argument!
He said he couldn't make the boy believe
He could find water with a hazel prong—
Which showed how much good school had ever done him.
He wanted to go over that. But most of all

160

He thinks if he could have another chance
To teach him how to build a load of hay—'

'I know, that's Silas' one accomplishment.
He bundles every forkful in its place,
And tags and numbers it for future reference,
So he can find and easily dislodge it
In the unloading. Silas does that well.
He takes it out in bunches like big birds' nests.
You never see him standing on the hay
He's trying to lift, straining to lift himself.'

'He thinks if he could teach him that, he'd be
Some good perhaps to someone in the world.
He hates to see a boy the fool of books.
Poor Silas, so concerned for other folk,
And nothing to look backward to with pride,
And nothing to look forward to with hope,
So now and never any different.'

Part of a moon was falling down the west,
Dragging the whole sky with it to the hills.
Its light poured softly in her lap. She saw it
And spread her apron to it. She put out her hand
Among the harp-like morning-glory strings,
Taut with the dew from garden bed to eaves,
As if she played unheard some tenderness
That wrought on him beside her in the night.
'Warren,' she said, 'he has come home to die:
You needn't be afraid he'll leave you this time.'

'Home,' he mocked gently.

                        'Yes, what else but home?
It all depends on what you mean by home.
Of course he's nothing to us, any more
Than was the hound that came a stranger to us
Out of the woods, worn out upon the trail.'

'Home is the place where, when you have to go there,
They have to take you in.'

                        'I should have called it
Something you somehow haven't to deserve.'

Warren leaned out and took a step or two,
Picked up a little stick, and brought it back
And broke it in his hand and tossed it by.
'Silas has better claim on us you think
Than on his brother? Thirteen little miles
As the road winds would bring him to his door.
Silas has walked that far no doubt today.
Why doesn't he go there? His brother's rich,
A somebody—director in the bank.'

'He never told us that.'

              'We know it though.'

'I think his brother ought to help, of course.
I'll see to that if there is need. He ought of right
To take him in, and might be willing to—
He may be better than appearances.
But have some pity on Silas. Do you think
If he had any pride in claiming kin
Or anything he looked for from his brother,
He'd keep so still about him all this time?'

'I wonder what's between them.'

               'I can tell you.
Silas is what he is—we wouldn't mind him—
But just the kind that kinsfolk can't abide.
He never did a thing so very bad.
He don't know why he isn't quite as good
As anybody. Worthless though he is,
He won't be made ashamed to please his brother.'

'I can't think Si ever hurt anyone.'

'No, but he hurt my heart the way he lay
And rolled his old head on that sharp-edged chair-back.
He wouldn't let me put him on the lounge.
You must go in and see what you can do.
I made the bed up for him there tonight.
You'll be surprised at him—how much he's broken.
His working days are done; I'm sure of it.'

'I'd not be in a hurry to say that.'

'I haven't been. Go, look, see for yourself.

162

But, Warren, please remember how it is:
He's come to help you ditch the meadow.
He has a plan. You mustn't laugh at him.
He may not speak of it, and then he may.
I'll sit and see if that small sailing cloud
Will hit or miss the moon.'

                        It hit the moon.
Then there were three there, making a dim row,
The moon, the little silver cloud, and she.

Warren returned—too soon, it seemed to her,
Slipped to her side, caught up her hand and waited.

'Warren?' she questioned.
                    'Dead,' was all he answered.

To a small boy who died at Diepkloof Reformatory

ALAN PATON

Small offender, small innocent child
With no conception or comprehension
Of the vast machinery set in motion
By your trivial transgression,
Of the great forces of authority,
Of judges, magistrates, and lawyers,
Psychologists, psychiatrists, and doctors,
Principals, police, and sociologists,
Kept moving and alive by your delinquency,
This day, and under the shining sun
Do I commit your body to the earth
Oh child, oh lost and lonely one.

Clerks are moved to action by your dying;
Your documents, all neatly put together,
Are transferred from the living to the dead,
Here is the document of birth
Saying that you were born and where and when,
But giving no hint of joy or sorrow,
Or if the sun shone, or if the rain was falling,
Or what bird flew singing over the roof
Where your mother travailed. And here your name

163

Meaning in white man's tongue, he is arrived,
But to what end or purpose is not said.

Here is the last certificate of Death;
Forestalling authority he sets you free,
You that did once arrive have now departed
And are enfolded in the sole embrace
Of kindness that earth ever gave to you.
So negligent in life, in death belatedly
She pours her generous abundance on you
And rains her bounty on the quivering wood
And swaddles you about, where neither hail nor tempest,
Neither wind nor snow nor any heat of sun
Shall now offend you, and the thin cold spears
Of the highveld rain that once so pierced you
In falling on your grave shall press you closer
To the deep repentant heart.

Here is the warrant of committal,
For this offence, oh small and lonely one,
For this offence in whose commission
Millions of men are in complicity
You are committed. So do I commit you,
Your frail body to the waiting ground,
Your dust to the dust of the veld,—
Fly home-bound soul to the great Judge-President
Who unencumbered by the pressing need
To give society protection, may pass on you
The sentence of the indeterminate compassion.

Bells for John Whiteside's daughter

JOHN CROWE RANSOM

There was such speed in her little body,
And such lightness in her footfall,
It is no wonder her brown study
Astonishes us all.

Her wars were bruited in our high window.
We looked among orchard trees and beyond
Where she took arms against her shadow,
Or harried unto the pond

The lazy geese, like a snow cloud
Dripping their snow on the green grass,
Tricking and stopping, sleepy and proud,
Who cried in goose, Alas,

For the tireless heart within the little
Lady with rod that made them rise
From their noon apple-dreams and scuttle
Goose-fashion under the skies!

But now go the bells, and we are ready,
In one house we are sternly stopped
To say we are vexed at her brown study,
Lying so primly propped.

(Thoughts written after reading of a mother's suicide)

E. S. BLUMENTHAL

Ay, those sad painful screams
   of a million brothers
   jumping out of their dreams,
   out of their minds,
   out of their eyes,
   out of a thousand books,
   out of a thousand poems,
   out of the day into the night.

and that scream that drowns
   in the wharves of a throat
and that sad scream of despair that
   is drowned in the silence of the air.

Ay, but worse, the scream
   of that mother that fell through
   a thousand sons into the
   open arms of a cold street,
   beneath the immensity of sky,
   beneath that tall concrete tree
   that reached heaven with a gasping cry.

When my father died

EDWIN BROCK

On the day my father died
  all the hoops in the neighbourhood rang
  skate wheels shrilled on summer pavements
  and I in my blakey-boots clanged one foot in each gutter

On the day my father died
  girls were running autumn-eyed, with wild hair
  and hands of silk; peg-tops had come round again
  and in the sky the angels were as plain as wings

But on the day my father died
  white faces fell from every window
  and every house found rooms of tears to hide
  while I, joy-jumping, empty-eyed sang on the day my father died

Now my father dies a little every day
And the faces from each window grow like mine

*The growing awareness of what his father's death means to the boy in that
poem is part of what must be among the most sensitive, difficult and sometimes
wonderful areas of a person's feelings — his relationships with those closest
to him:*

magnolia clinic

nigel v. fogg

on entering i threw my false voice
at you
and yours came back
across the sterilized distance.

smothered in a world of white
you were connected
by means of a long plastic tube
to a hole in the wall
labelled 'life'.

there were the usual questions
and your usual lies
and while mother continued
i turned to face the sets of eyes
watching the englishman's son.
i greeted them; 'hullo'.
which was neither here nor there.

through the window
there was a tree with leaves
and a bird,
and though late
traces of a long sun
unretreated among the park.

one day father
i suppose i shall turn
from the window
and find you withdrawn
into your hole in the wall
and turn again
to discover the bird gone
and the sun retreated
and mother and i shall leave
empty-lunged
walking
between shadow and shade
always

Fingers in the door

FOR KATE   DAVID HOLBROOK

Careless for an instant I closed my child's fingers in the jamb. She
Held her breath, contorted the whole of her being, foetus-wise, against
   the
Burning fact of the pain. And for a moment
I wished myself dispersed, in a hundred thousand pieces
Among the dead bright stars. The child's cry broke,
She clung to me, and it crowded in to me how she and I were
Light-years from any mutual help or comfort. For her I cast seed
Into her mother's womb; cells grew and launched itself as a being:
Nothing restores her to my being, or ours, even to the mother who
   within her
Carried and quickened, bore, and sobbed at her separation, despite all
   my envy,
Nothing can restore. She, I, mother, sister, dwell dispersed among dead
   bright stars:
We are there in our hundred thousand pieces!

Walking away

FOR SEAN

C. DAY LEWIS

It is eighteen years ago, almost to the day—
A sunny day with the leaves just turning,
The touch-lines new-ruled—since I watched you play
Your first game of football, then, like a satellite
Wrenched from its orbit, go drifting away

Behind a scatter of boys. I can see
You walking away from me towards the school
With the pathos of a half-fledged thing set free
Into a wilderness, the gait of one
Who finds no path where the path should be.

That hesitant figure, eddying away
Like a winged seed loosened from its parent stem,
Has something I never quite grasp to convey
About nature's give-and-take—the small, the scorching
Ordeals which fire one's irresolute clay.

I have had worse partings, but none that so
Gnaws at my mind still. Perhaps it is roughly
Saying what God alone could perfectly show—
How selfhood begins with a walking away,
And love is proved in the letting go.

Roy Kloof

SYDNEY CLOUTS

'Such a little king's eye', said my mother
who still had the kind imperial look.
'He'll command. Dear cherry-bright boy!'
Her faded English blood ran strong,
she dreamt of the shires all night long,
rose in the morning and called me, Roy.

That was the beginning. My father who came
raw from the veld with a rocky name,
though a mild man, frequently dreamt
that Circumstance galloped with him riding,
that History was thatched into his roof.
It hurt him to hear me christened, Roy Kloof.

168

Up behind father with little bright spurs
I dreamt I was galloping, gravely horsed.
I dreamt of a sceptre; I cried and I cried
till rock and shire were divorced.
Division incarnate! An unhappy role!
My country has given me flint for a soul.

Song of a Hebrew

DANNIE ABSE

Working is another way of praying.
You plant in Israel the soul of a tree.
You plant in the desert the spirit of gardens.

Praying is another way of singing.
You plant in the tree the soul of lemons.
You plant in the gardens the spirit of roses.

Singing is another way of loving.
You plant in the lemons the spirit of your son.
You plant in the roses the soul of your daughter.

Loving is another way of living.
You plant in your daughter the spirit of Israel.
You plant in your son the soul of the desert.

My parents kept me from children who were rough

STEPHEN SPENDER

My parents kept me from children who were rough
Who threw words like stones and who wore torn clothes.
Their thighs showed through rags. They ran in the street
And climbed cliffs and stripped by the country streams.

I feared more than tigers their muscles like iron
Their jerking hands and their knees tight on my arms.
I feared the salt coarse pointing of those boys
Who copied my lisp behind me on the road.

They were lithe, they sprang out behind hedges
Like dogs to bark at my world. They threw mud
While I looked the other way, pretending to smile.
I longed to forgive them, but they never smiled.

Some boys never feel like that, no matter what their circumstances, no matter what their parents do. Is Timothy Winters one of those children Stephen Spender's parents kept him from?

Timothy Winters

CHARLES CAUSLEY

Timothy Winters comes to school
With eyes as wide as a football-pool,
Ears like bombs and teeth like splinters:
A blitz of a boy is Timothy Winters.

His belly is white, his neck is dark,
And his hair is an exclamation-mark.
His clothes are enough to scare a crow
And through his britches the blue winds blow.

When teacher talks he won't hear a word
And he shoots down dead the arithmetic-bird,
He licks the patterns off his plate
And he's not even heard of the Welfare State.

Timothy Winters has bloody feet
And he lives in a house on Suez Street,
He sleeps in a sack on the kitchen floor
And they say there aren't boys like him any more.

Old Man Winters likes his beer
And his missus ran off with a bombardier,
Grandma sits in the grate with a gin
And Timothy's dosed with an aspirin.

The Welfare Worker lies awake
But the law's as tricky as a ten-foot snake,
So Timothy Winters drinks his cup
And slowly goes on growing up.

At Morning Prayers the Headmaster helves
For children less fortunate than ourselves,
And the loudest response in the room is when
Timothy Winters roars 'Amen!'

So come one angel, come on ten:
Timothy Winters says 'Amen
Amen amen amen amen.'
Timothy Winters, Lord.
                    Amen.

Can one say whether it is better to be a 'Stephen Spender' or a 'Timothy Winters'? Thom Gunn thinks one can — in a poem that is a reply to Spender's I think continually of those who were truly great *(p. 98) and* My parents kept me from children who were rough *(p. 169)* :

Lines for a book

THOM GUNN

I think of all the toughs through history
And thank heaven they lived, continually.
I praise the overdogs from Alexander
To those who would not play with Stephen Spender.
Their pride exalted some, some overthrew,
But was not vanity at last: they knew
That though the mind has also got a place
It's not in marvelling at its mirrored face
And evident sensibility. It's better
To go and see your friend than write a letter;
To be a soldier than to be a cripple;
To take an early weaning from the nipple
Than think your mother is the only girl;
To be insensitive, to steel the will,
Than sit irresolute all day at stool
Inside the heart; and to despise the fool,
Who may not help himself and may not choose,
Than give him pity which he cannot use.
I think of those exclusive by their action,
For whom mere thought could be no satisfaction—
The athletes lying under tons of dirt
Or standing gelded so they cannot hurt
The pale curators and the families
By calling up disturbing images.
I think of all the toughs through history
And thank heaven.they lived, continually.

A Negro sermon: Simon Legree

VACHEL LINDSAY

Legree's big house was white and green.
His cotton-fields were the best to be seen.
He had strong horses and opulent cattle,
And bloodhounds bold, with chains that would rattle.
His garret was full of curious things:
Books of magic, bags of gold,
And rabbits' feet on long twine strings,
But he went down to the Devil.

Legree, he sported a brass-buttoned coat,
A snake-skin necktie, a blood-red shirt.
Legree, he had a beard like a goat,
And a thick hairy neck, and eyes like dirt.
His puffed-out cheeks were fish-belly white,
He had great long teeth, and an appetite.
He ate raw meat, 'most every meal,
And rolled his eyes till the cat would squeal.
His fist was an enormous size
To mash poor niggers that told him lies:
He was surely a witch-man in disguise.
But he went down to the Devil.

He wore hip-boots, and would wade all day
To capture his slaves that had fled away.
But he went down to the Devil.
He beat poor Uncle Tom to death
Who prayed for Legree with his last breath.
Then Uncle Tom to Eva flew,
To the high sanctoriums bright and new;
And Simon Legree stared up beneath,
And cracked his heels, and ground his teeth:
And went down to the Devil.
He crossed the yard in the storm and gloom;
He went into his grand front room.
He said, 'I killed him, and I don't care.'
He kicked a hound, he gave a swear;
He tightened his belt, he took a lamp,

Went down cellar to the webs and damp.
There in the middle of the mouldy floor
He heaved up a slab; he found a door—
And went down to the Devil.

His lamp blew out, but his eyes burned bright.
Simon Legree stepped down all night—
Down, down to the Devil.
Simon Legree he reached the place,
He saw one half of the human race,
He saw the Devil on a wide green throne,
Gnawing the meat from a big ham-bone,
And he said to Mister Devil:
    'I see that you have much to eat—
    A red ham-bone is surely sweet.
    I see that you have lion's feet;
    I see your frame is fat and fine,
    I see you drink your poison wine—
    Blood and burning turpentine.'

And the Devil said to Simon Legree:
    'I like your style, so wicked and free.
    Come sit and share my throne with me,
    And let us bark and revel.'
And there they sit and gnash their teeth,
And each one wears a hop-vine wreath,
They are matching pennies and shooting craps,
They are playing poker and taking naps.
And old Legree is fat and fine:
He eats the fire, he drinks the wine—
Blood and burning turpentine—
    Down, down with the Devil;
        Down, down with the Devil;
            Down, down with the Devil.

Of course our reactions to people differ tremendously, depending not only on them and on ourselves but also on the way in which we come upon them. What reaction do we have to these two people?

To my mother

GEORGE BARKER

Most near, most dear, most loved and most far,
Under the window where I often found her
Sitting as huge as Asia, seismic with laughter,
Gin and chicken helpless in her Irish hand,
Irresistible as Rabelais, but most tender for
The lame dogs and hurt birds that surround her,—
She is a procession no one can follow after
But be like a little dog following a brass band.

She will not glance up at the bomber, or condescend
To drop her gin and scuttle to a cellar,
But lean on the mahogany table like a mountain
Whom only faith can move, and so I send
O all my faith and all my love to tell her
That she will move from mourning into morning.

The discardment

ALAN PATON

We gave her a discardment
A trifle, a thing no longer to be worn,
Its purpose served, its life done.
She put it on with exclamations,
Her eyes shone, she called and cried,
The great bulk of her pirouetted
She danced and mimed, sang snatches of a song.
She called out blessings in her native tongue
Called to her fellow-servants
To strangers and to passers-by
To all the continent of Africa
To see this wonder, to participate
In this intolerable joy.

174

And so for nothing
Is purchased loyalty and trust
And the unquestioning obedience
Of the earth's most rare simplicity.
So for nothing
The destruction of a world.

*How do we relate to other people, to people perhaps different from ourselves —
different in colour or nationality, or different simply because 'he's the man
next door'? (The first poem is written by a white Canadian in Trinidad.)*

Meeting of strangers

EARLE BIRNEY

'Nice jacket you gat deh, man!'

He swerved his bicycle toward my curb
to call   then flashed round the corner
a blur in the dusk   of somebody big
redshirted   young   dark   unsmiling

As I stood waiting for a taxi to show
I thought him droll at least
A passing pleasantry? It was frayed
a sixdollar coat   tropical weight
in this heat only something with pockets
to carry things in

Now all four streets were empty
Dockland   everything shut
It was a sound no bigger than a breath
that made me wheel

He was ten feet away   redshirt
The cycle leant by a post farther off
where an alley came in   What?!

My turning froze him
in the middle of some elaborate stealth
He looked almost comic   splayed
but there was a glitter
under the downheld hand
and something smoked from his eyes

175

By God if I was going to be stabbed
for my wallet (adrenalin suffused me)
it would have to be done in plain sight
I made a flying leap
to the middle of the crossing
White man   tourist   surrogate   yes
but not guilty enough
to be skewered in the guts for it
without raising all Trinidad first
with shouts   fists   feet   whatever
—I squared round to meet him

and there was a beautiful taxi
lumbering in from a sidestreet
empty!

As I rolled away   safe as Elijah
lucky as Ganymede
there on the curb I'd leaped from
stood that damned cyclist solemnly
shouting

'What did he say?' I asked the driver
He shrugged at the windshield
'Man dat a crazy boogoo
He soun like he say
"dat a nice jump you got too"'

The unexploded bomb

C. DAY LEWIS

Two householders (semi-detached) once found,
Digging their gardens, a bomb underground—
Half in one's land, half in t'other's, with the fence between.
Neighbours they were, but for years had been
Hardly on speaking terms. Now X unbends
To pass a remark across the creosoted fence:
'Look what I've got! . . . Oh, you've got it too.
Then what, may I ask, are you proposing to do
About this object of yours which menaces my wife,
My kiddies, my property, my whole way of life?'
'Your way of life,' says Y, 'is no credit to humanity.

176

I don't wish to quarrel; but since you began it, I
Find your wife stuck-up, your children repel me,
And let me remind you that we too have the telly.
This bomb of mine—'
               'I don't like your tone!
And I must point out that, since I own
More bomb than you, to create any tension
Between us won't pay you.'
               'What a strange misapprehension!'
Says the other: 'my portion of bomb is near
Six inches longer than yours. So there!'

'They seem,' the bomb muttered in its clenched and narrow
Sleep, 'to take me for a vegetable marrow.'

'It would give me,' said X, 'the very greatest pleasure
To come across the fence now with my tape-measure—'
'Oh no,' Y answered, 'I'm not having you
Trampling my flowerbeds and peering through
My windows.'

        'Oho,' snarled X, 'if that's
Your attitude, I warn you to keep your brats
In future from trespassing upon my land,
Or they'll bitterly regret it.'
               'You misunderstand.
My family has no desire to step on
Your soil; and my bomb is a peace-lover's weapon.'

Called a passing angel, 'If you two shout
And fly into tantrums and keep dancing about,
The thing will go off. It is surely permissible
To say that your bomb, though highly fissible,
Is in another sense one and indivisible;
By which I mean—if you'll forgive the phrase,
Gentlemen—the bloody thing works both ways.
So let me put forward a dispassionate proposal:
Both of you, ring for a bomb-disposal
Unit, and ask them to remove post-haste
The cause of your dispute.'

emphasise tragic/irony agree
— they can only have the bomb
that they must have the bomb

horrified

At the angel. 'Remove my bomb?' they sang
In <u>unison both</u>: 'allow a gang →*negative — allows people to deprive of the*
To invade my garden and pull up the fence *a gang*
Upon which my whole way of life depends? →*fear of opp. ideology.*
Only a <u>sentimental idealist</u> →*anti - nukes → romantic visionaries*

survived by emotion
suggest

Could moot it. I, thank God, am a realist.' →*sees things the way*
they really are
venied reason *sensibly worried*
The angel fled. The bomb turned over *→ & communist wouldn't see*
stupid *do* *that*
In its sleep and mumbled, 'I shall soon discover,
If X and Y are too daft to unfuse me,
<u>How the Devil</u> intends to use me.' →*explode into nuclear*
war

→ dialogue, rhyme, colloquialism] → emphasise the danger

*Does the difficult business of international relations become easier to under-
stand if one reads both that comic view by Cecil Day Lewis and* Mending wall *by Robert Frost (p. 59)?
Sometimes a sense of estrangement makes people feel very alone, lost, even
homeless:*

Journey through the night

JOHN HOLLOWAY

At the first hour from dawn
The traveller in the window seat
Rubbed his eyes, woke from a daze,
Brushed his rough hair back with great
Podgy fingers, gave a yawn,
Cleared the pane's white dewy haze,
Then stared so eagerly, it might
Have been his home place come in sight.

But at the second hour from dawn
The traveller in the window seat
Suddenly turned away from the world
As though he saw some thing too sweet
Or too bitter to be borne;
And when he met my glance, he curled
His body to the wall, and wept
I thought; but it may be he slept.

At the third hour from dawn
The ticket man rolled back the door:
The traveller blurted out that he
Wanted another ticket for
Some other place, somewhere further on;
He spoke shortly, confusedly;
But I saw he did not know,
Now, where in the world to go.

Lament of the banana man

EVAN JONES

Gail, I'm telling you, I'm tired fi true
Tired of Englan', tired of you.
But I can't go back to Jamaica now . . .

I'm here in Englan', I'm drawing pay!
I go to de undergroun' every day—
Eight hous is all, half-hour fo' lunch
M'uniform's free an' m' ticket-punch—
Punchin' tickets not hard to do,
When I'm tired of punchin', I let dem through.

I get a paid holiday, once a year.
Ol' age an' sickness can't touch me here.
I have a room of m' own, an' an iron bed,
A Dunlopillo under m' head,
A Morphy-Richards to warm de air,
A Formica table, an easy chair.
I have summer clothes, an' winter clothes,
An' paper 'kerchiefs to blow m' nose.

My yoke is easy, my burden is light
I know a place I can go to any night.

Dis place Englan'! I'm not complainin'
If it col', it col', if it rainin', it rainin'
I don' min' if it's mostly night,
Dere's always inside, or de sodium light.
I don' min' white people lookin' at me,
Dey don' want me here. Don' is deir country?

You won' catch me bawling any homesick tears
If I don' see Jamaica for a t'ousan' years!

Gail, I'm tellin' you, I'm tired fi true
Tired of Englan', tired of you
I can't go back to Jamaica now
But I'd want to die there . . . anyhow.

I years had been from home

EMILY DICKINSON

I years had been from home,
And now, before the door,
I dared not open, lest a face
I never saw before

Stare vacant into mine
And ask my business there.
My business,—just a life I left,
Was such still dwelling there?

I fumbled at my nerve,
I scanned the windows near;
The silence like an ocean rolled,
And broke against my ear.

I laughed a wooden laugh
That I could fear a door,
Who danger and the dead had faced,
But never quaked before.

I fitted to the latch
My hand, with trembling care,
Lest back the awful door should spring,
And leave me standing there.

I moved my fingers off
As cautiously as glass,
And held my ears, and like a thief
Fled gasping from the house.

Are the people in the last two poems able, in the first place, to define for themselves what lies at the bottom of their 'aloneness', their 'alienness'? or, in the second place, to communicate this to others?

The desire, the need, to communicate, to establish a meaningful relationship with others, to affect other people's lives and be affected by them, is basic to human beings. To want to communicate and feel unable to: this is something one has to try to resolve:

Cathedral

CHARLES ROM

I would they were not mine,
These thoughts that course within me.
Would someone else was governed thus
By the hot hand of chance,
Which halts for none and asks no pardon.
Yet I must build a vault,
That they might not escape
And be lost in the cruel clutch of time,
That greedy, grasping child that lies,
And kills the fleeting whispers
That float upon the sudden wind.
Surely these are mine alone?
The night and sea and sounds,
The love and ache of distance,
The murmur of my heart
When nothing stirs the waves within.
Yet, yet. Yet they will not be contained.
Like some twisting, writhing, drowning thing
They seek the air above,
To breathe and stretch and wash
In the streams of other men.
Reach out, reach out to touch
That golden glow
Which burns within some barren nook
Long hid by dreary drapes of rust
Behind which men must hide.
Yes, perchance I will forget,
Perchance my flame will die.
Yet have I built a spire
Which stands now like a beacon
To a winter's night when all was still.

I love you well

CHARLES ROM

I love you well
Whom love forbids
That I should ever tell.
You stand across
A phantom gate
I cannot break
With eunuch dreams.
My hand could reach
Yet never breach
The void 'tween
Fist and face.
Oh look once deep
And let me rest
One quiet sleep.
One sleep till
Rotting thought returns
Which bursts the fruit
And beauty burns.

Though I be young

CHARLES ROM

Though I be young
And you unknown
I know your heart
Oh song unsung.
Often we have talked
When silence screams
Often have you walked
My drifting dreams;
When fullness fled
Friend sorrow basks
Flicking a lash
Of licking lead.
Stand solid soon
Beside me here
Ere I deny you are;

182

Come soon, come soon
To crutch this soul
Oh strong yet distant
Star.

In fact, is love — or, at any rate, ideal love — even possible?

The song of wandering Aengus

WILLIAM BUTLER YEATS

I went out to the hazel wood,
Because a fire was in my head,
And cut and peeled a hazel wand,
And hooked a berry to a thread;
And when white moths were on the wing,
And moth-like stars were flickering out,
I dropped the berry in a stream
And caught a little silver trout.

When I had laid it on the floor
I went to blow the fire aflame,
But something rustled on the floor,
And some one called me by my name:
It had become a glimmering girl
With apple blossom in her hair
Who called me by my name and ran
And faded through the brightening air.

Though I am old with wandering
Through hollow lands and hilly lands,
I will find out where she has gone,
And kiss her lips and take her hands;
And walk among long dappled grass,
And pluck till time and times are done
The silver apples of the moon,
The golden apples of the sun.

He wishes for the cloths of heaven

Had I the heavens' embroidered cloths,
Enwrought with golden and silver light,
The blue and the dim and the dark cloths
Of night and light and the half-light,
I would spread the cloths under your feet:
But I, being poor, have only my dreams;
I have spread my dreams under your feet;
Tread softly because you tread on my dreams.

The effort of love

D. H. LAWRENCE

I am worn out
with the effort of trying to love people
and not succeeding.

Now I've made up my mind
I love nobody, I'm going to love nobody,
I'm not going to tell any lies about it
and it's final.

If there's a man here and there, or a woman
whom I can really like,
that's quite enough for me.

And if by a miracle a woman happened to come along
who warmed the cockles of my heart
I'd rejoice over the woman and the warmed cockles of my heart
so long as it didn't all fizzle out in talk.

Elemental

D. H. LAWRENCE

Why don't people leave off being lovable
or thinking they are lovable, or wanting to be lovable,
and be a bit elemental instead?

Since man is made up of the elements
fire, and rain, and air, and live loam
and none of these is lovable
but elemental,
man is lop-sided on the side of the angels.

I wish men would get back their balance among the elements
and be a bit more fiery, as incapable of telling lies
as fire is.
I wish they'd be true to their own variation, as water is,
which goes through all the stages of steam and stream and ice
without losing its head.

I am sick of lovable people,
somehow they are a lie.

A small, keen wind

THOMAS BLACKBURN

My wife for six months now in sinister
Tones has muttered incessantly about divorce,
And, since of the woman I'm fond, this dark chatter
Is painful as well as a bit monotonous.
Still, marvel one must, when she fishes out of that trunk,
Like rags, my shadier deeds for all to see
With 'This you did when sober, and that when drunk',
At the remarkable powers of memory.
For although I wriggle like mad when she whistles up
Some particularly nasty bit of handiwork,
The dirty linen I simply cannot drop,
Since 'Thomas Blackburn' is stitched by the laundry mark.
So I gather the things and say, 'Yes, these are mine,
Though some cleaner items are not upon your list',
Then walk with my bundle of rags to another room
Since I will not play the role of delinquent ghost

And be folded up by guilt in the crook of an arm.
I saw tonight—walking to cool the mind—
A little moonshine on a garden wall
And, as I brooded, felt a small, keen wind
Stroll from the Arctic at its own sweet will.

But, however at odds one may be with others and the world, reconciliation and Spring do eventually come — at first with tentative gestures, with tentative blades of grass. Then, with gathering momentum, love and Spring explode together in an exhilarating affirmation of life:

She tells her love while half asleep

ROBERT GRAVES

She tells her love while half asleep,
   In the dark hours,
      With half-words whispered low:
As Earth stirs in her winter sleep
   And puts out grass and flowers
      Despite the snow,
      Despite the falling snow.

Alba

EZRA POUND

As cool as the pale wet leaves
                of lily-of-the-valley
She lay beside me in the dawn.

Coming

PHILIP LARKIN

On longer evenings,
Light, chill and yellow,
Bathes the serene
Foreheads of houses.
A thrush sings,
Laurel-surrounded
In the deep bare garden,
Its fresh-peeled voice
Astonishing the brickwork.

It will be spring soon,
It will be spring soon—
And I, whose childhood
Is a forgotten boredom,
Feel like a child
Who comes on a scene
Of adult reconciling,
And can understand nothing
But the unusual laughter,
And starts to be happy.

in Just-

e. e. cummings

in Just-
spring   when the world is mud-
luscious the little
lame balloonman

whistles   far   and wee

and eddieandbill come
running from marbles and
piracies and it's
spring

when the world is puddle-wonderful

the queer
old balloonman whistles
far   and   wee
and bettyandisbel come dancing

from hop-scotch and jump-rope and

it's
spring
and
       the

            goat-footed

balloonMan   whistles
far
and
wee

if up's the word;and a world grows greener

e. e. cummings

if up's the word;and a world grows greener
minute by second and most by more—
if death is the loser and life is the winner
(and beggars are rich but misers are poor)
—let's touch the sky:
                    with a to and a fro
(and a here there where)and away we go

in even the laziest creature among us
a wisdom no knowledge can kill is astir—
now dull eyes are keen and now keen eyes are keener
(for young is the year,for young is the year)
—let's touch the sky:
                    with a great(and a gay
and a steep)deep rush through amazing day

it's brains without hearts have set saint against sinner;
put gain over gladness and joy under care—
let's do as an earth which can never do wrong does
(minute by second and most by more)
—let's touch the sky:
                    with a strange(and a true)
and a climbing fall into far near blue

if beggars are rich(and a robin will sing his
robin a song)but misers are poor—
let's love until noone could quite be(and young is
the year,dear)as living as i'm and as you're
—let's touch the sky:
                    with a you and a me
and an every(who's any who's some)one who's we

Shalom bomb

BERNARD KOPS

I want a bomb, my own private bomb, my shalom bomb.
I'll test it in the morning, when my son awakes,
hot and stretching, smelling beautiful from sleep. Boom! Boom!
Come my son dance naked in the room.
I'll test it on the landing and wake my neighbours,
the masons and the whores and the students who live downstairs.

Oh I must have a bomb and I'll throw open windows and
count down as I whizz around the living room,
on his bike with him flying angels on my shoulder,
and my wife dancing in her dressing gown.

I want a happy family bomb, a do-it-yourself bomb,
I'll climb on the roof and ignite it there about noon.
My improved design will gong the world and we'll all eat lunch.

My pretty little bomb will play a daytime lullaby and
thank you bomb for now my son falls fast asleep.
My love come close, close, the curtains, my lovely bomb, my darling,
my naughty bomb. Burst around us, burst between us, burst within
us. Light up the universe, then linger, linger
while the drone of the world recedes.

Shalom Bomb—

I want to explode the breasts of my wife. Ping! Ping!
In the afternoon and wake everyone,
to explode over playgrounds and parks, just as children
come from schools. I want a laughter bomb,
filled with sherbet fountains, liquorice allsorts, chocolate kisses,
candy floss,
tinsel and streamers, balloons and fireworks, lucky bags,
bubbles and masks and false noses.
I want my bomb to sprinkle the earth with roses.

I want the streets of the world to be filled with crammed, jammed
kids, screaming with laughter, pointing their hands with wonder,
at my lemonade ice-cream lightning and mouthorgan thunder.
I want a one-man-band bomb. My own bomb.

My live long and die happy bomb, my die peacefully old age bomb,
in our own beds, bomb.
My Om Mane Padme Hum bomb, my Tiddley Om Pom bomb,
my goodnight bomb, my sleeptight bomb,
my see you in the morning bomb,
I want my bomb, my own private bomb, my Shalom Bomb.

Snow

LOUIS MACNEICE

The room was suddenly rich and the great bay-window was
Spawning snow and pink roses against it
Soundlessly collateral and incompatible:
World is suddener than we fancy it.

World is crazier and more of it than we think,
Incorrigibly plural. I peel and portion
A tangerine and spit the pips and feel
The drunkenness of things being various.

And the fire flames with a bubbling sound for world
Is more spiteful and gay than one supposes—
On the tongue on the eyes on the ears in the palms of one's hands—
There is more than glass between the snow and the huge roses.

*Sometimes this sort of joyous celebration of life makes poets extend their being
at one with the world and with men to their God — sometimes a God not
precisely defined, sometimes a God with whom they identify closely:*

i thank You God for most this amazing

e. e. cummings

i thank You God for most this amazing
day:for the leaping greenly spirits of trees
and a blue true dream of sky;and for everything
which is natural which is infinite which is yes

(i who have died am alive again today,
and this is the sun's birthday;this is the birth
day of life and of love and wings:and of the gay
great happening illimitably earth)

how should tasting touching hearing seeing
breathing any—lifted from the no
of all nothing--human merely being
doubt unimaginable You?

(now the ears of my ears awake and
now the eyes of my eyes are opened)

The face on the Turin shroud

JAMES BRABAZON

This was the look of him? This down-to-earth man?
This convinces me. None of the flimsy faces
The painters put on him. This man never arrived
At resurrection without a hard won fight,
Nor was half air before he achieved ascension.
With him he took a look of the earth he lay in—
Rock, and a little soil, and old olive roots—
A sturdy, serene man, common sense in a riddle.
He looks like his talk, before it was pared by parsons,
Spun into sermons, and· so on, transtabulated
Into theology. This man is marvellous--
Death instinct with life, life at peace.
This is man.

They say he will judge me. I'm convinced.
I am judged already. I stand before him, knowing
That like each man I am my own disaster.
He knows I know. He will be merciful.
This man looks like all that I ask of God—
I can call him both me and master.

Legend

JUDITH WRIGHT

The blacksmith's boy went out with a rifle
and a black dog running behind.
Cobwebs snatched at his feet,
rivers hindered him,
thorn-branches caught at his eyes to make him blind
and the sky turned into an unlucky opal,
but he didn't mind.
I can break branches, I can swim rivers, I can stare out any spider I meet,
said he to his dog and his rifle.

The blacksmith's boy went over the paddocks
with his old black hat on his head.
Mountains jumped in his way,
rocks rolled down on him,
and the old crow cried, You'll soon be dead;
and the rain came down like mattocks.
But he only said
I can climb mountains, I can dodge rocks, I can shoot an old crow any
    day.
And he went on over the paddocks.

When he came to the end of the day the sun began falling.
Up came the night ready to swallow him,
like the barrel of a gun,
like an old black hat,
like a black dog hungry to follow him.
Then the pigeon, the magpie and the dove began wailing,
and the grass lay down to pillow him.
His rifle broke, his hat blew away and his dog was gone,
and the sun was falling.

But in front of the night the rainbow stood on the mountain
just as his heart foretold.
He ran like a hare,
he climbed like a fox,

192

he caught it in his hands, the colours and the cold—
like a bar of ice, like the columns of a fountain,
like a ring of gold.
The pigeon, the magpie and the dove flew up to stare,
and the grass stood up again on the mountain.

The blacksmith's boy hung the rainbow on his shoulder,
instead of his broken gun.
Lizards ran out to see,
snakes made way for him,
and the rainbow shone as brightly as the sun.
All the world said, Nobody is braver, nobody is bolder,
nobody else has done
anything to equal it. He went home as easy as could be
with the swinging rainbow on his shoulder.

On the move

THOM GUNN

'Man, you gotta Go.'

The blue jay scuffling in the bushes follows
Some hidden purpose, and the gust of birds
That spurts across the field, the wheeling swallows,
Have nested in the trees and undergrowth.
Seeking their instinct, or their poise, or both,
One moves with an uncertain violence
Under the dust thrown by a baffled sense
Or the dull thunder of approximate words.

On motorcycles, up the road, they come:
Small, black, as flies hanging in heat, the Boys,
Until the distance throws them forth, their hum
Bulges to thunder held by calf and thigh.
In goggles, donned impersonality,
In gleaming jackets trophied with the dust,
They strap in doubt—by hiding it, robust—
And almost hear a meaning in their noise.

Exact conclusion of their hardiness
Has no shape yet, but from known whereabouts
They ride, direction where the tyres press.
They scare a flight of birds across the field:
Much that is natural, to the wild must yield.
Men manufacture both machine and soul,
And use what they imperfectly control
To dare a future from the taken routes.

It is a part solution, after all.
One is not necessarily discord
On earth; or damned because, half animal,
One lacks direct instinct, because one wakes
Afloat on movement that divides and breaks.
One joins the movement in a valueless world,
Choosing it, till, both hurler and the hurled,
One moves as well, always toward, toward.

A minute holds them, who have come to go:
The self-defined, astride the created will
They burst away; the towns they travel through
Are home for neither bird nor holiness,
For birds and saints complete their purposes.
At worst, one is in motion; and at best,
Reaching no absolute, in which to rest,
One is always nearer by not keeping still.

Leather-jackets, bikes and birds

ROBERT DAVIES

The streets are noisy
with the movement of passing motors.
The coffee bars get fuller.
The leather-jacket groups begin to gather,
stand, and listen, pretending they are
looking for trouble.
The juke box plays its continuous
tune, music appreciated by Most.
The aroma of Espresso
coffee fills the nostrils and

the night.
Motorbikes pull up.
Riders dismount and join
their friends in the gang.
They stand, smoking, swearing,
playing with the girls;
making a teenage row.
They pretend not to notice the drizzle
falling out of the dark,
because you've got to be hard to
be a leather-jacket.
A couple
in a corner, snogging,
hope the motor lights will not be
dipped too much,
so that the others will see them.
They must all have recognition;
there must always be enough
leather-jackets around them,
the same as theirs.
The street lamp on the side
of the street shows the rain
for what it is—wet and cold.
But it does not show their faces
for what they are.

What are city people like? How are they different from the blacksmith's boy out in the country? To what extent does the city determine the sort of people they become? See how the following poems correspond with your view of city life and city people:

City people

ELAINE UNTERHALTER

I saw an old man
In a worn suit
With a cross on the lapel—
Sitting in a park,
waiting
for the end of the world.

I saw a woman
who smelt rich,
who talked without meaning,
who went shopping every Wednesday.
I saw a girl
looking for truth,
probing the cracks in the pavement.
I saw a doctor
who did not care.
I saw a lawyer
with cents for eyes.
I saw a cruel man.
I saw a kind man.
And all these people
meant something to somebody
but where is my truth?
what do I mean?

In a station of the metro

EZRA POUND

The apparition of these faces in the crowd;
Petals on a wet, black bough.

Florence: design for a city

ELIZABETH JENNINGS

Take one bowl, one valley
Assisted by hills to peace
And let the hills hold back the wind a little
Only turning the trees
Only dividing the shadows
With a simple movement of sun
Across the valley's face.

And then set cypresses up,
So dark they seem to contain their repeated shadows
In a straight and upward leap,
So dark that the sun seems to avoid them to show
How austere they are, stiff, admonishing gestures
Towards the city, yet also protective
To the deep houses that the sun makes more deep.

Here I say the mind is open, is freed;
Anchored only to frailest thoughts, we are
Triumphantly subdued to the light's full glare.
It is simple then to be a stranger,
To have a mind that is wide
To permit the city to settle between our thoughts,
And between those hills, and flower and glow inside.

Sunday morning

LOUIS MACNEICE

Down the road someone is practising scales,
The notes like little fishes vanish with a wink of tails,
Man's heart expands to tinker with his car
For this is Sunday morning, Fate's great bazaar;
Regard these means as ends, concentrate on this Now,
And you may grow to music or drive beyond Hindhead anyhow,
Take corners on two wheels until you go so fast
That you can clutch a fringe or two of the windy past,
That you can abstract this day and make it to the week of time
A small eternity, a sonnet self-contained in rhyme.

But listen, up the road, something gulps, the church spire
Opens its eight bells out, skulls' mouths which will not tire
To tell how there is no music or movement which secures
Escape from the weekday time. Which deadens and endures.

→lyric of passing of time

Song at summer's end

Garden of Eden → natural, innocent   *1904–1957 NZ*

A. R. D. FAIRBURN

Down in the park the children play *→ happy in spite of poverty*
→ emphasis — happy go lucky — now
rag-happy through the summer day *→poverty hasn't diminished ability to play*
with dirty feet and freckled faces,
laughing, fighting, running races. *→no bitterness — light, carefree rhythm/hymn*

→line 16 barefoot

197

Dull against the smoky skies
the summer's heavy burden lies,
leaden leaves on tired trees
lacking supple limbs like these (children)

The skyline shows the shape of life,
tomorrow's world of sweat and strife,
fifty stacks and one grey steeple.
Down the street come factory people,
folk who used to play on swings,
dodging chores and apron-strings
to wrestle on the grass and run
barefoot with the fleeting sun.

Some of the kids are sailing boats;
the first leaf drops unheeded, floats
and dances on the muddy pond.
Shadows from the world beyond
lengthen, sprawl across the park;
day rolls onward towards the dark.
From the clock-tower, wreathed in smoke,
Time speaks gravely, stroke on stroke.

*That last poem ends on an ominous note — almost, in fact, a death knell. The
prayer and the epitaph which follow as general comments on the twentieth
century are disquieting, to say the least, but are they without hope?*

A prayer for all my countrymen

Though now few eyes
can see beyond
this tragic time's
complexities,
dear God, ordain
such deed be done,
such words be said,

198

that men will praise
Your image yet
when all these terrors
and hates are dead:

   Through rotting days,
   beaten, broken,
   some stayed pure;
   others learnt how
   to grin and endure;
   and here and there
   a heart stayed warm,
   a head grew clear.

Epitaph

H. D. CARBERRY

I think they will remember this as the age of lamentations,
The age of broken minds and broken souls,
The age of hurt creatures sobbing out their sorrow to the rhythm of
   the blues—
The music of lost Africa's desolation become the music of the town.

The age of failure of splendid things,
The age of the deformity of splendid things,
The age of old young men and bitter children,
The age of treachery and of a great new faith.
The age of madness and machines,
Of broken bodies and fear twisted hearts,

The age of frenzied fumbling and possessive lusts—
And yet, deep down, an age unsatisfied by dirt and guns,
An age which choked by the selfishness of the few who owned their
   bodies and their souls,
Still struggled blindly to the end,
And in their time reached out magnificently
Even for the very stars themselves.

Epitaph *should, by the implication of its title, be the final poem in this selection.
But is one simply being naïve to suggest that something more positive exists
with which to conclude these statements by men and women of our time?
The Phoenix, a mythical bird of ancient Egypt, was reborn and rose triumphantly
out of its own ashes. Do the last two poems perhaps celebrate a new beauty
and dignity of steel and concrete rising out of the rubble?*

Crucifixion of the skyscraper

JOHN GOULD FLETCHER

Men took the skyscraper
And nailed it to the rock. Each nerve and vein
Were searched by iron hammers. Hour on hour,
The bolts were riveted tighter. Steel and stone
Did what they could to quench the fiery core
That blazed within. Till when the work was done,
Solid as a sepulchre, square-rooted to the rock,
The skyscraper, a well-polished tomb of hope,
Guarded by busy throngs of acolytes,
Shouldered aside the sun. Within its walls
Men laid a little gold.
                    But not yet dead
However long battered by furious life,
However buried under tons of frozen weight
That structure was. At night when crowds no more
Jostled its angles, but the weary streets
Of a worn planet stared out at the stars;
Its towering strength grown ghostly, pure, remote,
Lone on the velvety night in flights of gold
The tower rose. The skyscraper dripped light.

Prayers of steel

CARL SANDBURG

Lay me on an anvil, O God.
Beat me and hammer me into a crowbar.
Let me pry loose old walls.
Let me lift and loosen old foundations.
Lay me on an anvil, O God.
Beat me and hammer me into a steel spike.
Drive me into the girders that hold a skyscraper together.
Take red-hot rivets and fasten me into the central girders.
Let me be the great nail holding a skyscraper through blue nights into
   white stars.

Acknowledgements

I must thank the following for various sorts of assistance in compiling this anthology:

a number of my close friends (who will know who they are), who have been made to 'live with' the book from its conception;

the publishers and especially Mr John Burn Wood, whose total and tireless involvement in the making of the book has helped more than I can adequately acknowledge to give it its final shape and even its title;

Miss M. Laurie and Mr Ken Durham, who read and reported on the manuscript, and many of whose suggestions were adopted;

and my largely unwitting collaborators, my English classes over six years, on whom I have 'tried out' a vast number of the poems not usually prescribed or anthologized in South Africa.

Acknowledgement is made to the following for permission to use works which are their copyright: to Angus and Robertson Ltd for 'Legend' from *The Gateway* by Judith Wright; to A. A. Balkema Publishers Ltd for 'Cape Coloured batman' and 'Stranger to Europe' from *Stranger to Europe* by Guy Butler, and to Professor Guy Butler for his poem 'A prayer for all my countrymen', which appeared in *New Coin*; to Mr Thomas Blackburn for his poem 'A small, keen wind' from *A Breathing Space* published by Putnam and Co.; to Blackwood and Janet Paul Ltd for 'On the mountain' from *The Living Countries* by M. K. Joseph; to Mr E. S. Blumenthal for his poems 'The earth's atomic death' and '(Thoughts written after reading of a mother's suicide)'; to Mr James Brabazon for his poem 'The face on the Turin shroud' reprinted from *Modern Religious Verse* published by Studio Vista Ltd; to Jonathan Cape Ltd and the Hogarth Press for 'Come live with me', 'Let us now praise famous men' and 'A time to dance' from *Collected Poems 1954*, and 'Walking away' and 'The unexploded bomb' from *The Gate*, by Cecil Day Lewis; to Jonathan Cape Ltd for 'Naming of parts' from *A Map of Verona* by Henry Reed, and for 'In the snake park' and 'The wild doves at Louis Trichardt' from *Collected Poems*, and 'Shot at sight' from *Taste and Remember*, by William Plomer; to Curtis Brown Ltd for 'The serf', 'The Zulu girl', 'Horses on the Camargue' and 'Tristan da Cunha' from *The Collected Poems* by Roy Campbell published by The Bodley Head; to J. M. Dent and Sons Ltd and the trustees for the copyrights of the late Dylan Thomas for 'Fern Hill', 'Poem in October', 'Do not go gentle into that good night', 'The hunchback in the park' and 'And death shall have no dominion' from *Collected Poems 1934–1952* by Dylan Thomas; to André Deutsch Ltd for 'Florence: design for a city' from *A Way of Looking* by Elizabeth Jennings; to Mr C. J. Driver for his poem 'Transvaal afternoon', Part I of 'In the Lowveld', which appeared in *Groote Schuur* and *The Lion and the Impala*; to Eyre and Spottiswoode Ltd for 'Secretary bird' from *African Negatives* by Alan Ross; to Faber and Faber Ltd for 'Musée des Beaux Arts', 'Look, stranger',

'The unknown citizen' and 'Lay your sleeping head' from *Collected Shorter Poems 1927–1957* by W. H. Auden, for 'To my mother' from *Collected Poems* by George Barker, for 'Preludes', 'Journey of the Magi' and 'Triumphal march' from *Collected Poems 1909–1962* by T. S. Eliot, for 'Crucifixion of the skyscraper' by John Gould Fletcher, for 'On the move' and 'Lines for a book' from *The Sense of Movement*, and 'Considering the snail' from *My Sad Captains*, by Thom Gunn, for 'Hawk roosting' and 'Esther's tomcat' from *Lupercal*, and 'The horses' from *The Hawk in the Rain*, by Ted Hughes, for 'Meeting point', 'Prayer before birth', 'The sunlight on the garden', 'Snow' and 'Sunday morning' from *The Collected Poems of Louis MacNeice 1966*, for 'In a station of the metro' and 'Alba' from *Personae* by Ezra Pound, for 'An elementary school classroom in a slum', 'I think continually of those who were truly great' and 'My parents kept me from children who were rough' from *Collected Poems* by Stephen Spender; to the literary executors of the late A. R. D. Fairburn for his poem 'Song at summer's end', which appeared in *The Arts Year Book 1947* published by Whitcombe and Tombs Ltd; to Messrs Weissberger V. Frosch on behalf of Mrs Edgar Lee Masters for ' "Butch" Weldy' from *Spoon River Anthology* by Edgar Lee Masters published by T. Werner Laurie; to Mr Nigel V. Fogg for his poem 'magnolia clinic', which appeared in *English Alive 1968*; to Mr Robert Graves for 'In broken images', 'She tells her love while half asleep', 'The cool web' and 'Warning to children' from *Collected Poems 1965* by Robert Graves published by Cassell and Co. Ltd; to Rupert Hart-Davis Ltd for 'Timothy Winters' from *Union Street* by Charles Causley, and for 'Autumn on the land' from *Songs at the Year's Turning* by R. S. Thomas; to David Higham Associates Ltd for 'Blue umbrellas' from *Bread rather than Blossoms* by D. J. Enright published by Secker and Warburg; to Mr David Holbrook for his poem 'Fingers in the door' from *Imaginings* published by Putnam and Co., 1961; to Human & Rousseau Ltd for 'The gamblers' and 'Emerald dove' from *A Corner of the World* by Anthony Delius; to Hutchinson Publishing Group Ltd for 'Song of a Hebrew' from *Walking under Water* by Dannie Abse; to Miss Jenny Joseph for her poem 'Warning', which first appeared in *The Listener* and is reprinted from *New Poems 1965* published by Hutchinson and Co.; to Mr Bernard Kops and *Tribune* for 'Shalom bomb', which appeared in *Tribune* and is reprinted from *Erica I want to read you something* published by Scorpion Press; to Mrs H. R. Lake for 'Seed' by H. C. Bosman reprinted from *The Oxford Book of South African Verse*; to MacGibbon and Kee Ltd for 'anyone lived in a pretty how town', 'in Just-', 'what if a much of a which of a wind', 'i thank You God for most this amazing', 'r-p-o-p-h-e-s-s-a-g-r', 'somewhere i have never travelled' and 'if up's the word; and a world grows greener' from *The Complete Poems* by e. e. cummings, for 'Constantly risking absurdity' from *An Eye on the World* by Lawrence Ferlinghetti, for 'Proletarian portrait' and 'This is just to say' from *The Collected Earlier Poems*, and 'Heel & toe to the end' from *Pictures from Brueghel and Other Poems*, by William Carlos Williams; to Macmillan and Co. Ltd and the trustees of the Hardy Estate for 'In time of "the breaking of nations" ' from *The Collected Poems of Thomas Hardy*; to the Macmillan Company of New York for 'A Negro sermon: Simon Legree' from *The Collected Poems* by Vachel Lindsay, copyright 1917 by the Macmillan Company renewed 1945 by Elizabeth C. Lindsay; to the Marvell Press for 'Journey through the night' from *The Minute and Longer Poems* by John Holloway, and for 'Coming' and 'Toads' from *The Less Deceived* by Philip Larkin; to McClelland and Stewart Ltd, Toronto, for 'Meeting of strangers' from *The Collected Poems* by Earle

Index of Authors

Abse, 169
Aiken, 117
Anonymous, 1-3
Arnold, 51-2
Auden, 90-4
Barker, 174
Binyon, 59
Birney, 175-6
Blackburn, 185-6
Blake, 28-9
Blumenthal, 147-8, 165
Bosman, 150
Brabazon, 191
Brock, 166
Brooke, 69-71; 138
Browning, 47-51
Butler, 105-7; 136-7, 198-9
Campbell, 82-7
Carberry, 199
Causley, 170
Chaucer, 3-8
Cheek, 156
Clouts, 119, 125-6, 168-9
Coleridge, 35-7
cummings, 79-81; 123, 187-8, 190-1
Davies, 194-5
Dederick, 124-5, 144-5
Delius, 132, 150
Dickinson, 127-8; 130, 158, 180
Donne, 16-18
Drayton, 9
Driver, 134-5
Eliot, 71-5
Enright, 118
Fairburn, 197-8
Ferlinghetti, 116
Fletcher, 200
Fogg, 166-7
Frost, 59-64; 157-8, 158-63
Graves, 81-2; 115, 117, 186
Gray, 24-7
Gunn, 124, 171, 193-4
Hardy, 53
Herbert, 18-19
Herrick, 18
Holbrook, 167
Holloway, 178-9
Hopkins, 53-6
Housman, 56

Hughes, 107-9; 133
Jennings, 196-7
Jones, 179-80
Joseph, J., 153-4
Joseph, M. K., 143-4
Keats, 40-5
Kirkup, 141-2
Kops, 189-90
Larkin, 154-5, 186-7
Lawrence, 64-9; 134, 148-9, 151-3, 184-5
Levertov, 118-19
Lewis, 88-90; 168, 176-8
Lindsay, 172-3
Livingstone, 128, 130-1, 132, 135, 155
Lovelace, 21
MacNeice, 94-7; 190, 197
Magee, 140-1
Marlowe, 10-2
Marvell, 21-2
Masters, 156-7
Milton, 20
Owen, 75-9; 138-9
Paton, 163-4, 174-5
Pickett, 122
Plomer, 120-1, 128-9, 136
Pope, 22-4
Porter, 146-7
Pound, 186, 196
Raleigh, 12-3
Ransom, 164-5
Reed, 139-40
Rom, 181-2
Ross, 131
Sandburg, 148, 200
Shakespeare, 13-16
Shapiro, 126-7
Shelley, 37-9
Shirley, 19-20
Sidney, 9
Spender, 97-9; 169
Tennyson, 45-7
Thomas, D., 99-105
Thomas, R. S., 151
Unterhalter, 195-6
Whitman, 133-4
Williams, 121-2, 123
Wordsworth, 30-5
Wright, 192-3
Yeats, 56-8; 183-4

Index of Titles

A bird came down the walk, 130

A narrow fellow in the grass, 127

A Negro sermon: Simon Legree, 172

A prayer for all my countrymen, 198

A prayer in the Pentagon, 144

A small, keen wind, 185

A time to dance, 89

Accident, 156

After apple-picking, 60

After the opera, 148

Alba, 186

An elementary school classroom in a slum, 97

An Essay on Man, *From*, 23

An Irish airman foresees his death, 57

And death shall have no dominion, 99

Anthem for doomed youth, 77

anyone lived in a pretty how town, 79

At the round earth's imagin'd corners, 17

Auto wreck, 126

Autumn on the land, 151

Bat, 66

Bells for John Whiteside's daughter, 164

Birches, 62

Blue stuff, 135

Blue umbrellas, 118

'Butch' Weldy, 156

Cape Coloured batman, 105

Carrion comfort, 54

Cathedral, 181

City people, 195

Come live with me and be my love, 88

Coming, 186

Composed upon Westminster Bridge, 35

Considering the snail, 124

Constantly risking absurdity, 116

Crucifixion of the skyscraper, 200

Death be not proud, 16

Death, the leveller, 19

Do not go gentle into that good night, 103

Dover Beach, 51

Dulce et decorum est, 76

Edward, 1

Eight o'clock, 56

Elegy written in a country churchyard, 24

Elemental, 185

Emerald dove, 132

Epitaph, 199

Esther's tomcat, 133

Fern Hill, 104

Fingers in the door, 167

Florence: design for a city, 196

God's grandeur, 53

Greater love, 75

Hawk roosting, 107

Heaven, 69

Heel & toe to the end, 121

Helen of Kirconnell, 2

He wishes for the cloths of heaven, 184

High flight, 140

History, 59

Horses on the Camargue, 83

I love you well, 182

i thank You God for most this amazing, 190

I think continually of those who were truly great, 98

I years had been from home, 180

if up's the word; and a world grows greener, 188

In a station of the metro, 196

In broken images, 117

in Just-, 187

In the snake park, 128

In time of 'the breaking of nations', 53

Introduction to The Prologue to The Canterbury Tales, 3
Inversnaid, 54

Jerusalem, 29
Journey of the Magi, 73
Journey through the night, 178

Karroo stop, 125
Kubla Khan, 35

Lake morning in autumn, 130
Lament of the banana man, 179
Last lesson of the afternoon, 151
Lay your sleeping head, 93
Leather-jackets, bikes and birds, 194
Legend, 192
Let me not to the marriage of true minds, 15
Let us now praise famous men, 88
Leviathan, 128
Lines composed a few miles above Tintern Abbey, 31
Lines for a book, 171
Lizard, 134
London, 1802, 30
Look, stranger, 90

magnolia clinic, 166
Mantis, 124
Meeting of strangers, 175
Meeting point, 95
Mending wall, 59
Mountain lion, 68
Musée des Beaux Arts, 91
My last duchess, 47
My mistress' eyes are nothing like the sun, 16
My own heart let me have more pity on, 55
My parents kept me from children who were rough, 169
My true love hath my heart, 9

Naming of parts, 139
No more Hiroshimas, 141
Not marble, nor the gilded monuments, 15

Ode on a Grecian urn, 41
Ode to a nightingale, 42
Ode to the west wind, 37
On his blindness, 20
On the mountain, 143
On the move, 193
'Out, out—', 157

Peace, 138
Poem in October, 100
Poetry is death cast out, 119
Poverty, 149
Prayer before birth, 94
Prayers of steel, 200
Preludes, 71
Proletarian portrait, 123
Prospice, 51
Psalm of those who go forth before daylight, 148

Roy Kloof, 168
r-p-o-p-h-e-s-s-a-g-r, 123

Secretary bird, 131
Seed, 150
Shall I compare thee to a summer's day?, 13
Shalom bomb, 189
She tells her love while half asleep, 186
Shot at sight, 120
Snake, 64
Snow, 190
somewhere i have never travelled, 81
Song at summer's end, 197
Song of a Hebrew, 169
Song of Myself, From, 133
Stopping by woods on a snowy evening, 63
Strange meeting, 78
Stranger to Europe, 136
Sunday morning, 197
Sunstrike, 155

The best of school, 152
The bustle in a house, 158
The collar, 18
The cool web, 81
The death of the hired man, 158
The discardment, 174

208

The earth's atomic death, 147
The effort of love, 184
The face on the Turin shroud, 191
The gamblers, 150
The good morrow, 17
The hill, 70
The horses, 108
The hunchback in the park, 102
The king, 132
The laboratory, 49
The lamb, 28
The Miller, 6
The nymph's reply to the shepherd, 12
The one that got away, 122
The parting, 9
The passionate shepherd to his love, 11
The Rape of the Lock, *From*, 22
The second coming, 58
The secret, 118
The sentry, 138
The serf, 82
The song of wandering Aengus, 183
The sunlight on the garden, 96
The tiger, 28
The Tragical History of Doctor Faustus, *From*, 10
The unexploded bomb, 176
The unknown citizen, 92
The Wife of Bath, 5
The wild doves at Louis Trichardt, 136
The wild swans at Coole, 56
The world is too much with us, 30
The Zulu girl, 83
This image or another, 117
This is just to say, 122

Thou art indeed just, Lord, if I contend with thee, 55
Though I be young, 182
(Thoughts written after reading of a mother's suicide), 165
Timothy Winters, 170
Toads, 154
To a small boy who died at Diepkloof Reformatory, 163
To autumn, 40
To his coy mistress, 21
To Lucasta, going to the wars, 21
To my mother, 174
To the virgins, to make much of time, 18
Transvaal afternoon, 134
Tristan da Cunha, 85
Triumphal march, 74

Ulysses, 45

Walking away, 168
Warning, 153
Warning to children, 115
what if a much of a which of a wind, 80
When I have fears that I may cease to be, 45
When in disgrace with fortune and men's eyes, 14
When my father died, 166
When to the sessions of sweet silent thought, 14
Words between the Host and the Miller, 6

Your attention please, 146

-10 Poems - Dulce et Decorum · 70
To a Small boy at Depkloof Reform -10
.The Unexploded Bom - 176
The Parting .9
The Good . Morrow - 17
The World - 30
Kubla 85
Irishman - 56

14 October 1969
~~Gliwice~~   GLIWICE
Poland 2:00 am
20 January 1972.

4:00 am